INTARSIA KNITS

12 Colourful Knitwear Designs to Make Your Own

ANNA HUSEMANN

photography by Lena Scherer

quadrille

Contents

Introduction

Hello, I am Anna, a textile and knitwear designer based in Hamburg, Germany. My work is all about colour, shapes, and materials and how they interact with each other. I interpret the traditional craft of knitting in a modern, abstract way, taking a step back from small, repetitive motifs to instead create an expressive and pictorial character. In doing so, the intarsia technique is my favourite tool.

I grew up in a family of creative women. My great grandmother and my grandmother were both seamstresses and my mother is a passionate knitter. As a child they made me handmade clothes and toys and I learned to knit even before I went to school. I really like how craft binds us together and I enjoy every hour the women in my family spend together crafting.

During my textile design studies I was able to try many fields of textile design, such as weaving, knitting, screen-printing, embroidery, and pattern design. I soon specialized in the field of knitting and deepened my skills on the domestic knitting machine as well as my use of colours and materials. What I particularly like about knitting, and I think that is partly why I decided to focus on it, is that you can work experimentally, but your creations can still be used in everyday life.

For my master's graduation project, I knitted a series of illustrative, bold, and colourful knit samples inspired by nature and its organic forms. I spent one year drafting, designing and knitting on this project and concentrated on the intarsia technique for the first time. I was able to immerse myself deeply in this project and to work in a particularly experimental way. The knitted surfaces that I created still serve as a source of inspiration for new projects and some of them have inspired the knitting patterns in this book. Since graduating, I continued to delve deeper into the intarsia technique and, over the years, using intarsia to create motifs with bold abstract shapes has become my signature style.

I share a studio with my partner, who is a communication designer, but I am increasingly taking over the room with my three domestic knitting machines, lots of colourful yarns and all sorts of tools, including my mood boards. On these boards, I sort my thoughts and samples for ongoing projects and collect interesting shapes, notes, and materials that I come across in everyday life. This is where different projects come together and provide inspiration for one another and where new and interesting colour and textural combinations occur.

For a few years I used to sell knitted accessories made on my domestic knitting machine, and found there were two factors that had a strong influence on my design process – time and budget. What I love about designing knitting patterns, instead of items to make and sell, is that you can create something unique and adventurous without the need to prioritize such factors as production time. In addition, I find it particularly exciting to see how my designs are interpreted by knitters through their choice of colours and materials, and how this can completely change the look of a pattern.

This book provides an overview of my way of working, of creating colourful knitwear designs inspired by paper collages, of my favourite colour moods, fibres and shapes and all my tips and tricks for knitting with the intarsia technique. I want to help slow down today's fast-moving consumer society by creating colourful as well as eco-friendly individual pieces, and to encourage people to make their very own unique pieces of clothing and accessories, slowly and thoughtfully.

I hope this book will inspire you to get creative with knitting and to be experimental. And above all, have fun using the intarsia technique. Happy knitting!

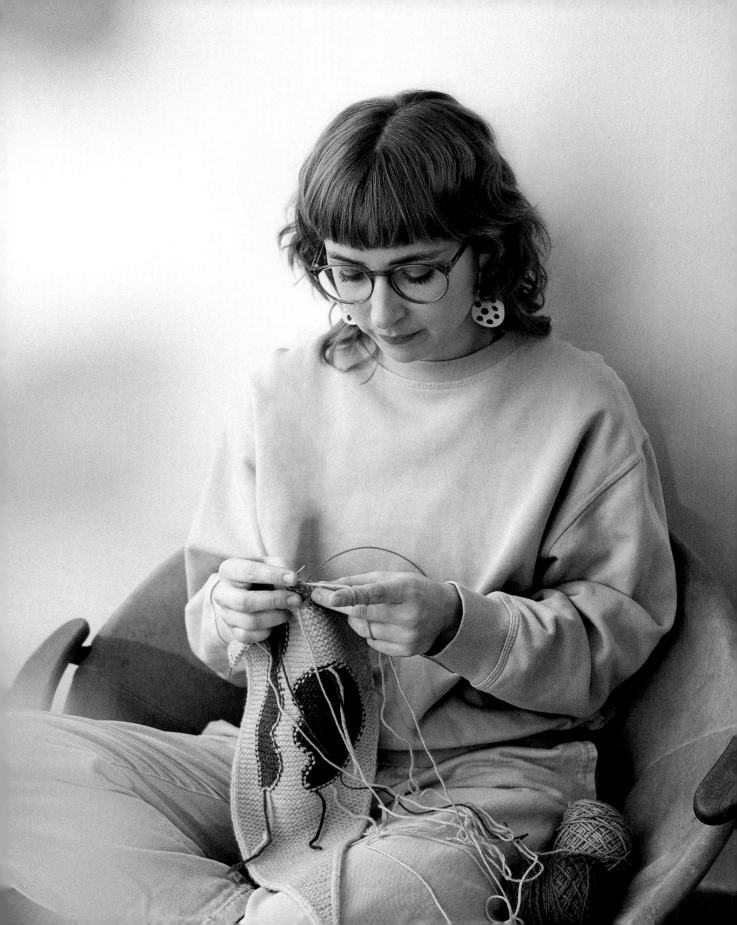

How I develop motifs

I am always on the lookout for interesting surfaces, structures, or textures that I can use as inspiration for my designs. My biggest source of inspiration is nature, especially the seaside. I am fascinated by organic forms such as leaves and berries, and textures like moss and lichen on bark, or the combination of beach grass growing through heather. In the natural world I find endless inspiration for motifs and compositions, as well as for beautiful colour combinations and special colour nuances.

It was during my master's degree in textile design that I discovered the collage technique for my work. For me, cutting paper collages is like sketching: I use them to sketch ideas for motifs, shapes, and compositions. By cutting out collages by hand, you create slightly imperfect, irregular shapes, which you set in relation to each other, creating overlays and negative forms. And as you create, you can edit and rearrange your shapes on the paper again and again until you are happy with the result. This way, you can create an overall pattern that is formed by individual shapes, and which is rich in variety.

Most of my collages are created on the spot, by capturing the mood of a landscape, scenery, or specific motifs in an abstract way.

First, I choose some suitable papers and colours. My papers are mostly hand painted to create exactly the colour shades that I prefer. These hand-painted papers add texture and vibrancy to my collages, similar to the impact of using iridescent or hand-dyed yarns in a knitting project.

Then, I look out for interesting details. I consciously decide which specific part of the scenery I want to capture, and which trees or plants seem to be important. I begin with the larger shapes first and then get into more detail. Being able to recognize the scenery or the specific shapes that inspire me is not always a given, as I do not create an exact image of the scenery. This gives me the creative freedom to adjust the composition, and to leave out or add shapes when cutting the collage.

The resulting illustration is more than just an abstract image of the scenery – it is, rather, a reflection of how I see, feel, and describe the scene in that specific moment. When I transform these illustrations into knitted textiles by filling their shapes with various materials, I am linking each textile project to the mood and the feel of the place where the collages were created.

Transforming paper collages into knit charts

Transforming sketches, or in my case paper collages, into knitting charts might seem mysterious, but it can be a relatively straightforward process. Below, I share my own process, which might provide some guidance for you to create your own designs.

My work process involves several steps that alternate between working manually and digitally. The process begins manually: new projects often begin with a series of hand-cut paper collage, that capture moods or specific shapes for a certain theme (see page 7).

I like to work with illustrative motifs rather than repeating patterns, and the intarsia technique is particularly suitable for transforming these illustrations into knitted textiles. It allows me to play with the motifs and their positioning more freely compared to any other multi-coloured knitting techniques.

After choosing suitable collages and shapes for my project, I scan them and trace them in Adobe Illustrator, which allows me to play around with the shapes and edit them to change their sizes and colours, and to try combining them in various ways. However, on the screen it can be difficult to get a good feel for how the sizes and proportions of the shapes will turn out on the finished item. What helps me here is to print out the shapes in their intended size, or roughly draw them on paper and cut them out, then physically arrange them on a piece of clothing, a hat or a scarf to try out how they fit best.

The next step in my design process is to find a suitable yarn for my design. Once found, I make some swatches to determine the tension (gauge), which is needed to transform my illustration into a pixel-based colour chart. This step is also digital, but luckily there are applications available that turn your illustration into a knit chart in seconds. I usually edit the chart afterwards to make it neat and, for example, make the shapes symmetrical or, indeed, to make them less symmetrical and more organic in nature.

And finally, I am ready to go back to manual for the last step – knitting! I take my yarn and needles and I follow the knit chart to create my own knitted illustration using the intarsia technique.

GETTING

STARTED

How to use this book

PROJECTS

This book contains knitting patterns for four garments, four accessories and four bags with different intarsia motifs. These motifs vary in the nature of their design, from graphic to organic.

SKILL LEVEL

There are patterns in this book to suit all skill levels. If you've never used the intarsia technique, there are lots of tips and tricks as well as step-by-step instructions so that intarsia beginners can also knit the projects. But there is plenty for even experienced intarsia knitters to discover as the designs play with variations of the technique and combine it with other knitting techniques.

Knitting patterns designated skill levels 1 and 2 are suitable for intarsia beginners but are also fun for intermediate knitters. Patterns at levels 3 and 4 are suitable for knitters with some previous knowledge, as they introduce specific techniques for which some experience is helpful. For the level 5 pattern, it is an advantage if you are already familiar with the techniques that are used, but because the pattern introduces these techniques one at a time, it is also suitable for less experienced but adventurous knitters who are eager to learn new techniques.

SIZING

All knitting patterns are available in different size ranges. The garments are size-inclusive and are available in nine sizes, which cover a bust-circumference of 76–156cm (30–61in). The headband and mittens are available in three sizes, depending on your head and hand circumference. The other accessories as well as the bags are one-size patterns, which can easily be varied in size depending on which yarn-weight you choose.

CHOOSING YOUR SIZE

The measurements for each size can be found in the notes at the start of each pattern, along with guidance, where applicable, on how to choose the best size for you.

For all garments you will need to measure your bust circumference. Measure at the widest part of your bust or chest. If you are in between two sizes, you can decide whether you prefer a tighter or a looser fit.

FIT

All garments are designed with positive ease, which means that the finished garment is larger than your body measurements. Positive ease allows freedom of movement and creates an oversized, boxy fit. Some of the garments are slightly cropped but can easily be lengthened as they are all knitted from the top down.

If you wish to lengthen or shorten the tee or sweater projects, you can do this easily when working the back by simply adding or leaving plain rows at the bottom. Bear in mind that, if you replicate the position of this length modification on the front, it will affect the positioning of the intarsia motif. A good way of shortening or lengthening the front is to add or reduce a roughly equal number of plain rows before and after the intarsia motif. Most importantly, ensure you adjust the position of the armhole increases accordingly, so that their positions remain the same as in the unmodified pattern.

TENSION (GAUGE)

Always knit a tension swatch before you start a new project to determine which needle size will help you obtain the correct tension, especially if you want to create a nice fitting garment.

Note: I am a tight knitter. If you tend to knit loosely, you probably may need to go down in needle size to match my tension.

What is also particularly important is to ensure you soak and block your swatch before measuring it, as this will give you a precise result.

RIGHT AND LEFT SHOULDERS

In the written instructions, "right shoulder" refers to the shoulder that covers your right shoulder when wearing the garment, and "left shoulder" refers to the shoulder worn on your left.

SPECIAL TECHNIQUES

At the beginning of each pattern, you will find notes outlining which special techniques are used in the pattern. These note may include instructions for specific stitches (bobble stitch, for instance) as well as details on how to achieve the required edge stitches. In these notes you will also find information on which intarsia techniques are used and, where necessary, you will be guided to the step-by-step sequences showing how to use those techniques.

GENERAL ABBREVIATIONS

On the inside front cover you will find a list of the abbreviations used in the knitting patterns in this book.

HOW TO READ KNIT CHARTS

Knit charts are an essential part of the intarsia technique. These are pixel-based diagrams that show, stitch by stitch and row by row, which colour to knit when. One box in the knit chart represents one stitch in your knitting project. A row of these boxes represents a row of stitches.

Follow your knit chart row by row. In order not to lose track, you can use a chart reader (see page 14) or track your progress online or in knitting apps.

Sometimes knit charts can feel intimidating, especially those designed for the intarsia technique, which can become rather large. For me, following a knit chart is relaxing, as it counts the rows for me, and it shows my progress clearly. Intarsia charts can also be kind of addictive – when I see a motif on a chart, I want to see how it will knit up, and I enjoy watching the shapes grow as I work.

In General: Knit charts are always read from the bottom up. You can use the thicker lines in the chart (which appear after every fifth stitch) as a guide to make counting stitches and rows on the chart faster.

How you read the knitting charts in this book varies depending on which type of stitch pattern you are using.

Below, I explain the differences.

1. **Stocking (stockinette) stitch:** The colours used to create the motif can change in both right-side and wrong-side rows. In the knit chart, read each right-side row from right to left, and each wrong-side row from left to right.

2. **Garter stitch:** I create my garter stitch designs so that the motif changes only on right-side rows, to obtain a neat colour change. So, the colourwork on each wrong-side row is identical to the right-side row directly preceding it. Therefore, you only need one chart row to represent each two rows of knitting (a right-side and the following wrong-side row). Read right-side rows from right to left, then read the same row from left to right for the wrong-side row.

3. **Brioche:** The knit charts for the Along The Coast Vest are read like a stocking (stockinette) stitch chart: reading right-side rows from right to left, and wrong-side rows from left to right. As the intarsia technique is used only with contrast colours, these are the only rows that are indicated in the chart. Therefore, you need to add one plain row in your main colour, after each chart row.

4. **Slip stitch:** As the slip stitch patterns used in the book also contain garter stitch elements, the slip stitch charts are read like garter stitch charts: always read right-side rows from right to left, and add an identical wrong-side row by reading the same chart row from left to right. The chart for the Full of Flowers Bag is an exception because you also knit two rows in your main colour after a right-side and wrong-side row indicated in the chart.

Tip: With each knit chart for pieces made using garter stitch, brioche or slip stitch, you will find a note with details explaining the reading direction.

Tools

Most of the tools I use daily are common knitting tools, but there are some that are particularly helpful for knitting intarsia. My favourite tool is a chart reader, which is basically a magnetic board that makes following your knit chart easier. Print out or copy your chart, attach it to the reader using magnets and use the magnetic ruler to track your rows.

Tip: Place the ruler *above* the row you want to knit next (rather than below it), so that you can see how the motif has changed since the previous row.

Another indispensable tool is my blocking mat. I block everything I knit, including swatches and experiments. Spread out a wet item on a blocking mat neatly, pin it to the mat and allow it to dry naturally so it dries in shape. There is no need to stretch out a garment before pinning unless you need to obtain the correct measurements.

I use circular needles in general when knitting, which are great for larger projects. If you are knitting narrow projects, such as headbands, bags, purses or scarves, you can use double-pointed needles or straight needles. As they do not have a cable joining them, yarns are less likely to tangle if knitting with multiple colours.

I usually wind up several balls of one colour when knitting intarsia, but tools such as bobbins (see page 24) can be helpful for handling the yarns.

MY TOOL LIST

Below is a list of tools that find useful.

1. **Circular needles** for larger knitting projects.

2. **Double-pointed needles (DPNs) or straight needles** for smaller knitting projects.

3. **Darning needles** are large, blunt needles used for closing the seams and weaving in the yarn ends.

4. **Measuring tape** for measuring tension (gauge) and your knitted item.

5. **Yarn scissors** for cutting the working yarn or the yarn ends.

6. **Blocking pins** for temporarily pinning together for a try-on, and for pinning while blocking.

7. **Stitch holder cords or leftover yarns** for placing stitches on hold while you work on another section of the piece.

8. **Crochet hook** for casting on using the provisional cast on method.

9. **Stitch markers** allow you to mark specific stitches, for instance, the stitches of a thumb.

10. **Removable markers** mark a specific point in a project, for example the end of the armhole increases.

11. **Chart reader** for following knit charts manually (see photo on page 158).

12. **Blocking mat** for blocking your knitwear (see photo on page 158).

Yarns and fibres

When I design a new product or create a new pattern, I spend hours thinking about colour combinations and material choices, as besides the motif, these are the most important aspects for me.

As a maker, I want to be responsible with materials I select to work with. So, I set myself some guidelines, in order to design thoughtfully made products with an eco-friendly and sustainable approach.

One of these guidelines, for example, which I have followed strictly for a few years, is to use only natural materials. In every step of the pattern or product development, from designing to shipping, I try to think of ways to avoid using or to replace plastic. If I choose to work with silk, for example, I use bourette or wild silk to try to ensure it is cruelty-free and that the fibres were collected after the worms have turned into moths. And I always choose organic cotton or recycled cotton over conventional cotton.

My favourite fibre to work with is 100 per cent sheep's wool. Besides all the impressive characteristics wool comes with, I just like how it feels while wearing it.

I try to integrate more and more local sheeps' wool into my projects, as I want to support the use of local wool. I like wool with a slightly rustic feel, as I prefer firmer, more compact knitted fabrics. For me, yarns with a slightly greyish base fibre are particularly interesting. They often create a moody colour palette, a bit like self-painted papers, where the different mixed shades can be paired beautifully.

Selecting the yarns for each project in the book was a carefully undertaken labour of love. It was not only important that the colours and fibres matched my design idea but, above all, that the values of the yarn companies matched mine, and that the fibres were sourced in ways that were ethical and cruelty-free.

Of course, every knitter has their own yarn preferences, and I encourage you to choose alternative yarns for your knitting projects. When looking for alternatives, compare the metreage (yardage) and characteristics of the yarns and always check your selections by knitting a tension (gauge) swatch.

HOW TO MATCH YARNS

One aspect of the intarsia technique that I really like is that, for motifs with multiple colours and small shapes, you only need a small amount of each colour. This is the perfect opportunity to dive deep into your yarn stash to use up leftover yarns from previous projects, deadstock yarns, flea market finds or hand-me-downs. This not only supports the conscious use of resources but can also give your project a unique character, as pairing leftovers can create interesting and unexpected colour and material combinations.

Working with leftovers feels great, but it can also be challenging to match the yarn weights when you are, for example, missing the banderole or the yarn brand.

Some designs play with yarns of different weights, but if you are aiming for the same yarn weight, there is a simple trick to find out if and how your choice of yarns might work well together.

1. Pick two yarns and loop them around each other so that both ends are doubled, and they intersect in the middle.

2. Holding each yarn double, twist its two strands together tightly, twisting evenly on either side of the intersection. Now compare the thicknesses of each doubled-and-twisted yarn to check how similar they are.

Some yarns look quite similar, but their actual yarn weight (and, therefore, how they knit up) also depends a lot on what material they are made of and how they are spun. This trick will help you to determine whether or not yarns are of a similar-enough weight to be used together when necessary.

Try to play around with your leftovers to make them more alike in thickness. You can hold them double or triple, or if one yarn is only slightly thinner, add a lace-weight strand of wool, mohair, or alpaca to it.

1.

2.

Using colour cards

When designing products and patterns, I use colour cards – also known as yarn wrappings – to help me create interesting colour combinations and material contrasts. Colour cards are basically cardboard strips, which are wrapped with small quantities of several yarns. Use them to place yarns of different colours, fibres, and sizes adjacent to one another on a single card, so you can see them together in isolation to get a good feel for how well they work together. You can use them to try out your ideas for different colour moods, to make a record of your favourite colour palettes and tonal combinations, or just simply brainstorm for your next project.

BRAINSTORMING COLOUR MOODS

You may approach a project with a clear idea of the colourway you intend to use for it. Or you may have a vague idea, or no idea at all! Colour cards can help you make decisions by trying out ideas, and unravelling and starting again until you establish a colourway you are excited about.

Choose one or two shades to start with, then decide on an approach before you continue. Do you want a warm or a cool colour palette? Do you prefer bold and vibrant hues or subtle shades with less contrast? Do you want to combine similar colours from the same colour family to create a monochromatic colour palette, or would you prefer complementary colours? Do you like pairing subtle natural tones with one or two contrasting shades? Do you want to create a gradient out of two or three shades? Do you like rich, deep earthy tones, or soft and dreamy pastels? Do you like a clean, minimalistic colour palette with classic colour combinations, such as black, grey, ivory, or off-white?

Choose the next colour according to your preferred approach, adding one colour after another. If, at a certain point, you no longer like a shade, remove it and replace it with a new colour.

This way you can create unique colour moods, depending on which approach you are following. The colour cards shown opposite (bottom row, right) all began with the same shade of apricot, then each one developed in a completely different direction depending on the approach I had in mind each time.

Composition: If you want to create colour cards for a specific motif, take a closer look at the tonal values in the original object of your inspiration (say, a landscape). If you choose shades that are similarly light or dark to the corresponding shapes in the original, the composition will have a similar effect, even if the colour mood is completely different.

MAKING COLOUR CARDS

You will need the following tools to create your own colour cards:
- leftover yarns of different colours and fibres
- thick paper or cardboard, cut into several cards. I like to work with cards which are approximately 1.5–3.5cm (½–1¼in) wide.
- scissors
- paper tape

1. Place the yarn end of your first colour diagonally across the back of your card as shown. Now wrap the yarn neatly around the card, securing the yarn end to the card beneath the wrapped yarn.

2. Wrap until you like the size of your colour strip, then cut the yarn. Secure this yarn end to the back of your card with paper tape, which makes handling and rearranging colours easier.

Repeat Steps 1 + 2 with your next colour directly next to the first wrap, continuing in this way until you have completed your colour card.

1.

2.

Using the intarsia technique

Intarsia is my favourite of all the knitting techniques! Unlike other colourwork techniques, such as stranded colourwork or working with stripes, intarsia allows you to combine bold organic shapes in your designs. The technique is used for knitting rather large, illustrative motifs, which are most frequently placed as individual (rather than repeated) elements. However, you can also fill an entire surface with intarsia motifs.

If you've knitted in intarsia before, you already know that you need patience for untangling all the balls of yarn used to create the various fields of colour. But I feel it is well worth the effort, because intarsia enables a spontaneity and irregularity that I love to work with.

INTARSIA VS STRANDED COLOURWORK

Understanding the difference between the intarsia technique and stranded colourwork (another technique that uses multiple colours in one piece of work) will help you gain a better understanding of intarsia. The differences are both visual (in the types of motifs each technique is best suited to creating) and practical (how yarns are used and managed to create the motifs).

STRANDED COLOURWORK (OPPOSITE PAGE, TOP)

Motifs in stranded colourwork consist of repeated patterns. This means that the same motif is repeatedly across the surface of the knitted fabric. The identical shapes have been placed next to each other over and over again.

Usually, two or three colours are used in a single row, and colours change after a few stitches. Each colour is carried across the wrong side of the work from the last stitch it was used to knit to the next stitch that is knitted in that colour. So, for stranded colourwork, you only need to work with one ball of yarn in each colour that appears in a single row to knit that row.

Carrying yarns across the wrong side in this way creates multiple floats with all the yarns you are using on the wrong side of your fabric.

When designing motifs for stranded colourwork, it is important to ensure that the floats on the wrong side do not become too long. This means that the motifs in stranded colourwork are often quite small, with the same colour appearing close to the last point it was used, often because the pattern is repeated.

INTARSIA (OPPOSITE PAGE, BOTTOM)

When motifs have large and/or isolated areas of colour, intarsia is the right technique to use. Unlike with stranded colourwork, for intarsia you use a separate ball of yarn for each colour field, and colours are not usually carried across the wrong side of the work. So, even if you use the same colour further along in your row, instead of carrying that colour across the wrong side as you would in stranded colourwork, you use two balls of the same colour on the same row – or as many as needed!

I do sometimes carry the yarn only a few stitches to the left or right, depending on how neat the wrong side of my fabric needs to be (see pages 28–29). For larger changes in the motif, e.g. more than 6–8 stitches (depending on the thickness of the yarn), I recommend cutting the yarn and reattaching it in the new position.

Having multiple balls of yarn can be intimidating for some knitters, but it has a great advantage. As you don't carry your yarn on the wrong side of the work, you do not have to pay attention to the length of the floats when designing motifs, which gives you a lot of creative freedom. You can play freely with the positioning of your motif. For instance, you can develop an abstract pattern that completely covers your garment, or you can place a motif only on the front or the back. Or you can highlight a specific part of your garment with just a few intarsia shapes.

But, when designing motifs for intarsia or choosing a pattern to follow, keep in mind that the more complex a design gets, the more balls are needed per row. Therefore, when choosing your project, try to adapt the complexity of the design to your intarsia experience.

Tip: Before you begin knitting your intarsia project, take a closer look at the pattern's motif and colour chart to count the fields of colour and verify how many balls are needed for each colour. If you do not have enough individual balls, divide a ball and wind as many mini-balls from it as you need.

WORKING FLAT VS WORKING IN THE ROUND
Another difference between the stranded colourwork and the intarsia technique is that, when working in stranded colourwork, you keep carrying all your yarns to the left as you knit. This makes working in the round possible, because each colour you need has travelled across the knitting with you on the wrong side, so it is right there on the wrong side of your work when you need to use it. Indeed, stranded colourwork is often knitted in the round.

When working in intarsia on fields of colour, you use one ball of yarn to work each field of colour from right to left on a right-side row, then from left to right on a wrong-side row, then back again. This makes it impossible to knit in the round, because the yarn for each colour field will have been left on the wrong side of the colour field. Consequently, intarsia is knitted flat. But, of course, there are exceptions in both cases.

INTARSIA VARIATIONS
What I find particularly interesting is to combine intarsia with other knitting techniques to create interesting modifications and variations. This way, you can create charming knit fabrics in which different colours, yarns, and fibres come together in unexpected ways. The following intarsia variations are used in the knitting patterns in this book.

Stocking (stockinette) stitch intarsia: This is probably the best-known way of working in intarsia. It creates a beautiful smooth surface with bold fields of colour.

Garter stitch intarsia: My favourite variation is garter stitch intarsia. As intarsia is most often knitted flat, it is easy and relaxing to work knit stitches only. Garter stitch ridges add texture to your motifs and keep the edges of each shape nice and neat.

Marled intarsia: I particularly like combining marling with intarsia to create motifs with a marled, two-tone effect. Here you can work with exciting fibre/yarn-type combinations and create motifs with a more subtle colour scheme. This technique is well suited for intarsia beginners, as fewer balls of yarn are required compared with regular intarsia.

Slipped stitch intarsia: By combining the intarsia technique with a slip stitch pattern, you can create interesting textures that add three-dimensionality to your multicoloured motifs.

Brioche intarsia: In this variation, intarsia meets two-coloured brioche, which results in a particularly exciting combination of three-dimensional ribs, vertical coloured lines, and colourful motifs.

Seamless intarsia: In this variation the intarsia technique is knitted without seams, which is suitable for garments or accessories where a seam would appear bulky. Further details on this technique can be found on page 31.

Yarn management

Intarsia is not a particularly difficult technique to learn or to knit with. But, depending on your motif, you will knit with 2–10 balls at the same time and, sooner or later, these will get tangled. So, be prepared to show some patience when knitting intarsia, and don't allow the number of balls involved in your project to make you feel nervous.

Depending on what type of person you are, I can recommend either of two approaches. Either embrace the chaos and knit a few relaxing rows without paying attention to what is happening to the balls of yarn, then take some time to sort everything out again. Or, if the tangling balls makes you nervous, untangle everything after each row, or every other row, so that all the balls of yarn stay organized.

There are a few tricks and tools that help with intarsia yarn management. They all come with pros and cons, so feel free to try them out and see which work best for you.

1. **Turning:** This technique works well if you are working with just a few balls and, ideally, with straight needles without a cable. It is not ideal for complex motifs with lots of colours. Place your balls, all organized, on a surface in front of you in the same order as in your knitting project. After knitting a right-side row, all your stitches are on the right needle. To turn the needle to work on the wrong side, turn it clockwise (or anticlockwise). After finishing the wrong-side row, turn the needle holding all the stitches anticlockwise (or clockwise). After finishing that wrong-side row, the yarns will be organized again! Note that it does not matter which direction you turn the needle after the first right-side row, as long as you turn it in the opposite direction after the wrong-side row, and keep alternating the directions for alternating rows.

2. **Yarn ends:** For small motifs, such as small dots, I prefer to use short pieces of yarn that hang down as loose ends. If they get tangled, you can simply pull them out of the tangle, as they are not wound into a ball. It is not easy to estimate the exact amount of yarn needed, but in the knitting patterns in the book I give an approximate amount of how many metres (and yards) of yarn are needed for each shape.

3. **Vessels:** I prefer to work on the couch because, this way, all balls can lie around me, and they can't unroll or drop down onto the floor. When I'm working at the table, I like to use small vessels, such as glasses or bowls, to hold the balls of yarn. That way they cannot roll off the table and I can organize them again more easily.

4. **Bobbins:** Another helpful tool for yarn management are bobbins. They are available in different versions: round or square, made of silicone, plastic, or wood. What they all have in common is that you can wind your yarn onto them and then fasten it, which has the advantage that the yarn does not unwind by itself and therefore does not get tangled up as much. Using bobbins also makes your knitting project easier to transport as you do not necessarily need a working surface. When working with bobbins, make sure that the yarn remains short up to the bobbin, otherwise there is a risk of the bobbins becoming tangled among themselves.

5. **Butterfly bobbins:** For complex designs with many colours, the bobbins may add extra weight to your knitting project. Alternatively, you can wind your yarn into butterflies. They have the same function as bobbins because the yarn is fastened and does not unwind by itself. However, you cannot wind them up again if you have unwound too much yarn.

Tip: If you are holding two or more strands together for your working yarn, wind the different strands together into a single ball before you begin, to prevent these strands from becoming tangled.

4.

5.

4.

3.

2.

Intarsia join

To avoid creating detached fields of colour when knitting intarsia, yarns are twisted when changing colour to create a regular intarsia join that keeps adjacent colour fields physically joined.

Note: When making an intarsia join, the yarns are always twisted on the **wrong side** of your work. Therefore, no matter which stitch you are knitting, always ensure both yarns are positioned at the wrong side before twisting them.

For example, when knitting garter stitch intarsia on a wrong-side row, you need to move the working yarn to the wrong side (currently at the front) to twist it with the new colour, then move the new colour to the right side (currently at the back) to continue knitting.

TWIST THE YARNS AS FOLLOWS

1. Ensure both yarns are at the WS of your work, moving one of them if necessary.

2. When dropping the old colour (the one that you just knitted with), lay it over the new colour (the one that you will be knitting with next).

3. Lift the new colour, so that it comes around the old colour from behind and underneath it.

4. Continue knitting, using the new colour.

Neat stitches: After twisting and knitting the first stitch in your new colour, pull both yarns slightly to avoid having large stitches at the edges of each motif.

Joining a new colour: On the first row of a new motif, or when adding new colours, no yarns are twisted. Simply drop the old colour, take the new colour and start knitting the number of stitches indicated in the chart.

Holes: Don't be confused when a hole appears below a new shape where you added a new colour. It will disappear once you weave in all ends, but take care to pull these ends tight when you knit the first row above it to avoid creating large stitches.

1.

↑ ON RS ROW
(LOOKING AT THE WS)

1.

↑ ON WS ROW

2.

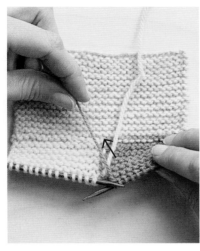

3.

4.

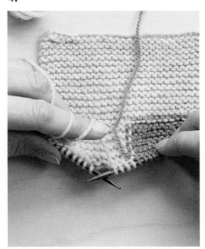

2.

3.

4.

Carrying yarns and binding floats

As the motif you are working on changes shape, you will need to carry yarns along the wrong side of the work for a few stitches to their correct positions in the charted pattern. This creates little floats on the wrong side of the work. These can be hidden, so that the wrong side is visually neat and tidy, and so that there are no floats that your fingers might catch easily as you put on or remove the item. How you hide the floats differs depending on whether you are carrying yarns towards the left or towards the right.

CARRYING YARNS TOWARDS THE LEFT

Use this technique when you need to carry the yarn a few stitches to the left to where you will next need it. In the example shown here, the green area needs to extend 8 stitches into the area currently in apricot, after which the apricot yarn will be used again, so the apricot yarn is carried 8 stitches to the left.

1. Using the working yarn (green), knit to the point at which you wish to begin carrying the apricot yarn. Drop your working yarn on the wrong side of the work, then lay the yarn you want to carry to the left (apricot) over the working yarn.

2. Pick up your working yarn (green) from behind the carried yarn (apricot) and knit the next stitch. You have used the working yarn to trap the carried yarn neatly against the WS of the work.

3. Repeat Steps 1 and 2 until you reach the point in the chart at which the colour change occurs, then drop the old working yarn (green) and continue in the new working yarn (apricot).

In the charts in this book, carrying yarn to the left is indicated by a left-facing arrow. You can twist the working and carried yarn after each stitch, after every other stitch, or after every third stitch, as you prefer. In the charts, I suggest how often to twist the yarns, which is indicated by a horizontal line across the two stitches between which the yarns should be twisted.

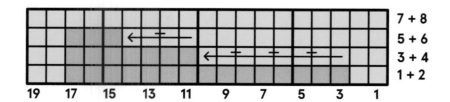

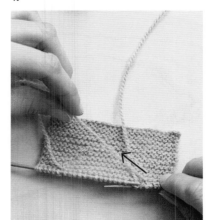

1.

2.

3.

↑ CARRYING YARN TO THE LEFT

CARRYING YARNS TOWARDS THE RIGHT

Use this technique when the yarn for the colour you need to use is a few stitches further along the row than you have reached so far, so you need to carry that strand a few stitches to the right. In the example shown here, the green yarn needs to be carried to the right by 5 stitches, into the area currently in apricot, then used to knit to the end of the row.

1. When you reach the first stitch that needs to be worked in the carried (green) yarn, pull the green strand along the wrong side of the row to bring it behind the tips of the needles and make an intarsia join (see pages 26–27) with the yarn you've been working with (apricot). Now drop the old working yarn (apricot) and knit the next stitch with the new working yarn (green). Note that you have made a float on the wrong side by carrying the green yarn to the right.

2. Before knitting the next stitch, pick up the float with the tip of the left needle. Insert the right needle into, first, the next stitch, then the picked-up float beside it on the left needle, and knit them together. Knit the next stitch.

3. Repeat Step 2 until you reach the end of the float. With every other stitch, you have trapped (or bound) the float neatly across the wrong side.

In the charts in this book, carrying the yarn to the right is indicated by a right-facing arrow. In some patterns, I indicate that you can leave the float unbound for two or three stitches. In the charts, I use a horizontal line to indicate when/where to bind the float.

1.

2.

3.

↑ CARRYING YARN TO THE RIGHT

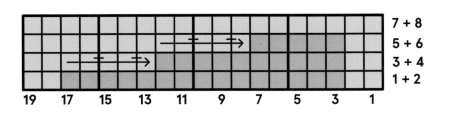

Intarsia cast on using multiple colours

In some projects, the motifs appear to extend beyond the edges of the knitted piece. In such cases you need to cast on using multiple colours in order to continue the intarsia colour pattern into the edges of the piece. To avoid having detached fields of colour in the cast on, which makes the first row harder to handle, connect the colours as follows:

1. Use the long-tail cast on method to cast on the number of stitches described in the pattern in the first colour. When you need to change colours, leave both ends of the old colour hanging down. Take the new colour, measure out the long tail needed for the number of stitches in the second colour and lay the tail around both strands of the old colour.

2. Pick up the new colour, pull all threads tight and continue working the long-tail cast on using the new colour.

1.

2.

Seamless intarsia

In workshops I am often asked if it is possible to knit with the intarsia technique in the round. It is possible, but I prefer to call it seamless intarsia. This is because, although you are creating a knit project without a seam, unlike with knitting in the round, you do not knit constantly in one direction – which is clockwise for most knitters – continuing past the beginning-of-round marker in the same direction. Instead, when you reach the marker you begin working anticlockwise on the wrong-side row. So, when using seamless intarsia, you are actually knitting back and forth across the rows, just as you do when knitting flat.

However, the work is joined in the round so that it is seamless. To do this, you need to ensure that you have two separate balls of yarn for each field of colour that flanks the marker – even if those fields of colour are, in fact, the same colour! This enables you to create a wrap at the marker (see pages 90–91) that keeps the work joined in a tube shape.

There is a straightforward reason for why you cannot continue working clockwise in the round when working with intarsia. If you did, when you reach any colour field, the yarn you need to use to work it would have been left on the other side of the colour field, where you last used it. By working wrong-side rows anticlockwise in seamless intarsia, you will always return to the last place you used each colour.

There are different techniques for knitting seamless intarsia, but the one I share in this book is a technique that I have discovered for myself. It achieves a simple, almost invisible join that looks like a regular intarsia join on the wrong side. The technique is unusual at first, but once you have got the hang of it, it is easy to implement.

WHEN TO USE SEAMLESS INTARSIA

The seamless intarsia method lends itself very well to certain projects, but it has its advantages and disadvantages. It is always worth weighing up, for each specific project, whether it makes sense to knit flat or seamless.

For instance, I made a double-layered reversible hat design, which was knitted in aran (worsted weight) yarn. Using seamless intarsia worked well because, had I knitted the hat flat, a seam would have been too bulky. In the Along the Coast Vest knitting pattern, the seamless intarsia technique is used for the ribbing, which allows the intarsia motif to continue at the ribs without the need to add a seam to the rib.

There are cases where I would not recommend using seamless intarsia. If, for example, you have a very colourful motif, and you are knitting both the front and back of the garment simultaneously using the seamless intarsia technique, you would have many more balls of yarn hanging from your work than you would have if working the back and front separately. This could slow down your knitting process rather than speeding it up.

Additionally, in some projects, such as bags, a seam can be useful as it provides stability.

If you decide to knit one of the designs in the book using the seamless intarsia method instead of knitting it flat, I recommend that you choose one side of the garment as the beginning of the round and work the yarn wrap (shown on pages 90–91) there with two balls of the main colour, using one ball on each side of the beginning-of-round (BOG) marker. I also recommend that you place a marker opposite the BOG marker to indicate the start of the second side, and work a yarn wrap with two balls of the main colour there, too. This joins the work into a tube on both sides, which replaces the side seams and, at the same time, creates symmetry.

PROJ

ECTS

Before Bloom Bandana

My local botanical gardens are a unique place with a
charming atmosphere. No matter what time of year
I visit, I encounter fascinating sights, sounds and
smells. I was inspired to design the motif for this cosy
bandana-shaped scarf by a visit during late spring,
during which I enjoyed the organic shapes of the
berries and leaves, the bold colour palettes of the
flowerbeds, and the tantalizing promise of the flower
buds – some still closed, others just opening.

#beforebloombandana

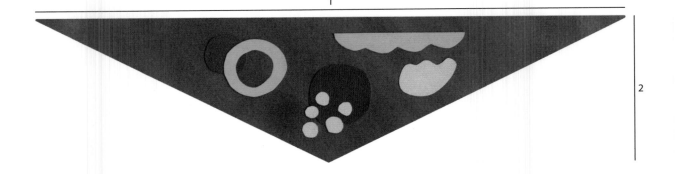

CONSTRUCTION

The Before Bloom Bandana is a small triangular scarf knitted in garter stitch in combination with the intarsia technique. The motif places organic shapes at the centre of the triangle. The triangle is knitted from the right-side corner to the left-side corner, first increasing and then decreasing on every other RS row along the left edge only to create the third point of the triangle (the lower point shown in the schematic above). An I-cord edge is worked along both sides as you knit for neat edges.

SKILL LEVEL
●●○○○

FINISHED MEASUREMENTS
1. **Width, measured point to point:** 96.5cm (38in)
2. **Depth:** 23cm (9in)

YARN
4-ply (fingering weight) yarn that matches the tension (gauge) in 4 shades. As the shapes in the motif use only a small amount of yarn, this is a great project for using up leftover odds and ends in your yarn stash.

MC: 200m (219yds)
CC1: 36m (40yds)
CC2: 32m (35yds)
CC3: 36m (40yds)

Yarn used in the samples shown opposite: John Arbon Textiles Knit by Numbers 4ply Mini skeins (50 per cent Merino, 50 per cent Bluefaced Leicester, 100m / 109yds, 25g / ⅞oz).

Colourway for sample 1 (opposite; back, right):
MC: KBN118, 2 skeins
CC1: KBN17, 1 skein
CC2: KBN60, 1 skein
CC3: KBN45, 1 skein

Colourway for sample 2 (opposite; front, centre):
MC: KBN17
CC1: KBN118
CC2: KBN45
CC3: KBN60

SAMPLE 1

SAMPLE 2

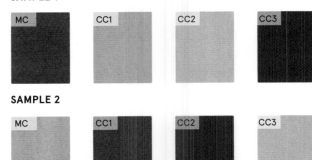

NEEDLES
3mm (US 2.5) circular needles, or size needed to obtain the correct tension (gauge).

TENSION (GAUGE)
26 sts x 48 rows to 10 x 10cm (4 x 4in) in garter stitch, measured after washing and blocking.

READING THE CHARTS
The chart shows only RS rows. The intarsia pattern for each odd-numbered row is exactly the same for the following even-numbered row. So, for rows 1 and 2, read the chart row labelled 1 + 2 from right to left for row 1 (RS), then from left to right for row 2 (WS), and so on. Note also that increases and decreases are made only on RS rows. So, symbols on the chart indicating increases and decreases refer to the RS rows (odd-numbered rows) only.

SPECIAL TECHNIQUES

INTARSIA JOIN
See pages 26–27.

CARRYING YARNS AND BINDING FLOATS
See pages 28–29.

I-CORD EDGE STITCH
First 3 sts of every row: K1, sl1p wyif, k1.
Last 3 sts of every row: Sl1p wyif, k1, sl1p wyif.

PATTERN
Cast on **6 sts.**
Set-up Row (WS): Work *K1, sl1p wyif* 3 times.
Row 1 (RS): K1, sl1p wyif, kfb, sl1p wyif, k1, sl1p wyif (1 st increased – 7 sts).
Row 2 (WS): K1, sl1p wyif, k2, sl1p wyif, k1, sl1p wyif.
Rows 3 + 4: Repeat Row 2. (**7 sts** in total)

INCREASE ROWS

To shape your bandana, increase 1 st at the end of every second RS row, directly before the sts for the I-cord edge.

Row 1 (RS): K1, sl1p wyif, k1, k to the last 4 sts, kfb, sl1p wyif, k1, sl1p wyif (1 st increased – 8 sts).

Row 2 (WS): K1, sl1p wyif, k to the last 3 sts, sl1p wyif, k1, sl1p wyif.

Row 3 + 4: Repeat Row 2.

Repeat Rows 1–4 a further 30 times. (**38 sts** in total)

Begin working **Chart 1** (see opposite) to create the intarsia pattern in garter stitch while, *at the same time*, repeating increase rows 1–4 until you reach the widest point (rows 101–104), at which point you will have **64 sts**. **Note:** See page 37 for notes on reading the charts before you begin following Chart 1.

DECREASE ROWS

On **Row 105 (RS)** begin decreasing 1 st at the end of every second RS row, again directly before the I-cord edge sts, as follows, while, *at the same time*, working Chart 1 to continue creating the intarsia pattern:

Row 1 (RS): K1, sl1p wyif, k1, knit to the last 5 sts, ssk, sl1p wyif, k1, sl1p wyi. (1 st decreased)

Row 2 (WS): K1, sl1p wyif, k1, knit to the last 3 sts, sl1p wyif, k1, sl1p wyif.

Rows 3 + 4: Repeat Row 2.

After finishing Chart 1, cut CC3, and continue knitting using MC only. Repeat decrease Rows 1–4 as above, but without changing colours, a further 33 times, until you have 7 sts remaining.

Final decrease row (RS): K1, sl1p wyif, ssk, sl1p wyif, k1, sl1p wyif (1 st decreased).

Cast (bind) off the remaining sts using your preferred method, for example the standard cast off.

FINISHING

Sew in all ends, for example by using the duplicate stitch method on the WS. Gently wash your Before Bloom Bandana and block it according to the measurements.

CHART 1

Note: See page 37 for notes on reading this chart before you begin following it.

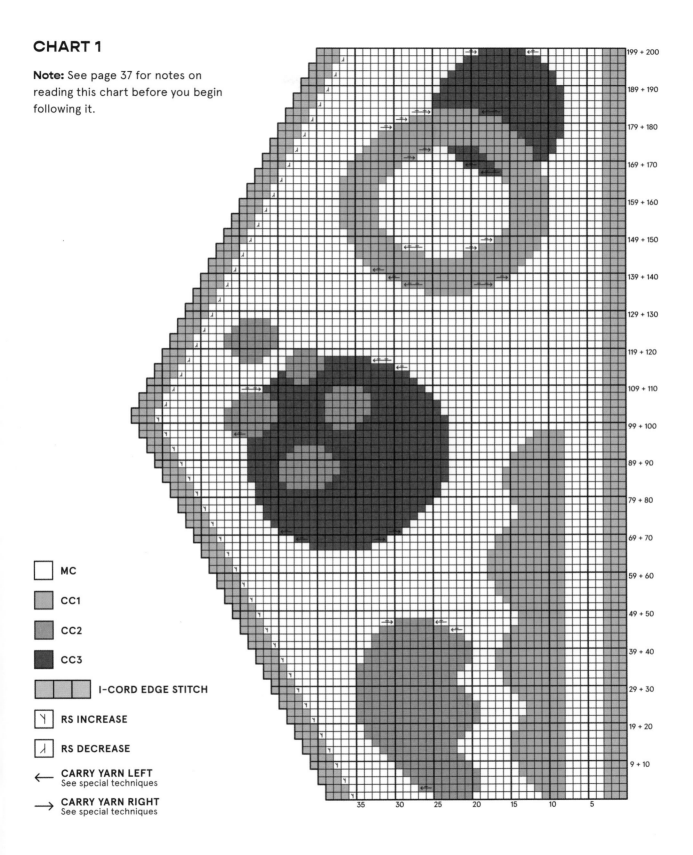

MC

CC1

CC2

CC3

I-CORD EDGE STITCH

RS INCREASE

RS DECREASE

← CARRY YARN LEFT
See special techniques

→ CARRY YARN RIGHT
See special techniques

For Small Things purse

This cute and versatile little purse is perfect for all kinds of small items. I use it for carrying change to buy ice cream on a beach day, but I will also pop in useful bits of crafting kit like small scissors and stitch markers to add to whichever bag I'm using to hold my current knitting project. If you're travelling or heading to the park, this purse is ideal for stashing your sweets or a deck of cards, and for a creative trip out, use it to carry your pens and a mini notebook. If you need to carry larger items, simply make it bigger!

#forsmallthingspurse

FLAT, UNFINISHED

FINISHED, FROM EITHER SIDE

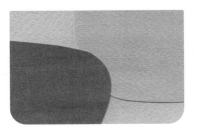

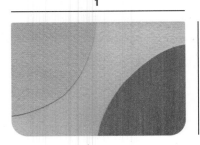

CONSTRUCTION

The For Small Things Purse is worked flat in a slip stitch textural pattern, which creates three-dimensional textured stripes as well as a firm fabric that is suitable for bags. The intarsia technique is also used, creating two botanical shapes using three colours.

The purse is knitted in one rectangle and folded in half. You knit the first side of the purse with an I-cord edge along both sides while following Chart 1 (see page 47) for the intarsia colour pattern. You then decerease the I-cord edge sts and work the second side with a garter stitch edge while following Chart 2 (see page 47) for the intarsia pattern. After finishing both sides, you work an I-cord cast (bind) off all the way around, then sew together the side seams. Next, you attach a zipper, followed by a cotton ribbon to hide the zipper seam.

SKILL LEVEL

FINISHED MEASUREMENTS

This purse can be knitted in various weights of yarn, such as 4-ply (fingering weight), DK (light worsted) or aran (worsted), meaning this pattern can result in various sizes. Measurements of finished purse in the suggested yarn:
1. **Length:** 15cm (6in)
2. **Height:** 11cm (4¼in)

YARN

Heavy weight DK or lightweight aran (worsted weight) yarn in a blend of wool and plant fibres for strength. As the purse uses only a small amount of yarn, this project is perfect for stash busting. You will also need waste yarn for casting on.

MC: 33m (36yds)
CC1: 33m (36yds)
CC2: 25m (28yds)

Yarn used in the sample: De Rerum Natura Robinson (70 per cent Organic merino d'Arles (France) and 30 per cent recycled cotton, including 2 per cent of other recycled fibres), 250m (270yds) per 100g (3½oz).
MC: pêche melba, 1 skein
CC1: azur, 1 skein
CC2: grand bleu, 1 skein

ZIPPER

Use a zipper suitable for the size of your finished purse. Zipper for the suggested yarn: 14cm (5½in) long

COTTON RIBBON

1.5cm (½in) wide, approx. 50cm (19½in) long, or to suit the size of the finished purse.

NEEDLES

3.75mm (US 5) circular needles, or size needed to obtain the correct tension (gauge).

TENSION (GAUGE)

26 sts x 46 rows to 10 x 10cm (4 x 4in) in the slip stitch pattern, measured after washing and blocking.

Knit a swatch in the slip stitch pattern to determine which needle size you need to achieve the correct tension. For the tension swatch, work the slip stitch pattern as follows: Cast on a multiple of 5 sts plus 2 sts, using the long-tail cast on method.
Set-up Row (WS): Repeat *k2, sl1p wyif, k1, sl1p wyif* to the last 2 sts, k2.
Row 1 (RS): Sl1k, k1, repeat *k1, sl1p wyif, k3* to the end of the row.
Row 2 (WS): Sl1k, k1, repeat *sl1p wyif, k1, sl1p wyif, k2* to the end of the row.
Repeat Rows 1 + 2 until your swatch is big enough for checking the tension.

Note: Stitches are counted from the RS, counting 3 stitches for each slip stitch stripe as well as 2 rows for each garter stitch ridge.

READING THE CHARTS

The charts show only RS rows. The intarsia pattern for each odd-numbered row is exactly the same for the following even-numbered row. So, for rows 1 and 2, read the chart row labelled 1 + 2 from right to left for row 1 (RS), then from left to right for row 2 (WS), and so on.

SPECIAL TECHNIQUES

INTARSIA JOIN
See pages 26–27.

CARRYING YARNS AND BINDING FLOATS
See pages 28–29.

SLIP STITCH PATTERN
The slip stitch pattern combines a garter stitch background with vertical lines in slipped stitches. Each vertical stripe consists of 3 stitches. On a RS row, the second stitch is slipped and, on a WS row, the first and third stitches are slipped, which pushes the 3 stitches together into a protruding vertical stripe.

I-CORD EDGE STITCH
First 3 sts of every row: K1, sl1p wyif, k1.
Last 3 sts of every row: Sl1p wyif, k1, sl1p wyif.

GARTER STITCH EDGE STITCH
First st of every row: Sl1k.
Last st of every row: K1.

PATTERN

SECTION 1
Using waste yarn, cast on **43 sts** using a provisional cast on method.
Change to CC1. Leaving a 30cm (12in) tail for the side seam later, knit as follows:
Set-up Row (WS): Using CC1, work *p3, k2* six times. Change to MC and, leaving a tail of approximately 1m (39½in) for the I-cord cast (bind) off later, work *p3, k2* two times, p3. You now have **30 sts in CC1** and **13 sts in MC**.

Begin working **Chart 1** (see page 47) to create the intarsia colour pattern while, *at the same time*, creating the slip stitch textural pattern by repeating rows 1 + 2 as follows:
Row 1 (RS): Repeat *k1, sl1p wyif, k3* to the last 3 sts, sl1p wyif, k1, sl1p wyif.
Row 2 (WS): K1, sl1p wyif, k1, repeat *k2, sl1p wyif, k1, sl1p wyif* to the end of the row.
Note: See left for notes on reading the charts before you begin following Chart 1.

DECREASE ROWS
After finishing Chart 1, decrease the first and last 3 sts of the row as follows, while changing the colours to repeat the colour changes of the previous row:
Row 1 (RS): K1, k2tog, k1, pass the first and second st on your right needle over the third st, k1, repeat *k1, sl1p wyif, k3* to the last 3 sts, k2tog, k1. Slip the last 3 sts on your right needle back onto your left needle, and pass the second and third st over the first st. Slip this st back onto your right needle (6 sts decreased). You now have **37 sts** remaining.

Row 2 (WS): Sl1k, k1, repeat *sl1p wyif, k1, sl1p wyif, k2* to the end of the row, changing the colours as in the previous row.

SECTION 2

Begin working **Chart 2** (see page 47) to create the intarsia colour pattern while, *at the same time*, working the slip stitch textural pattern with garter stitch edges by repeating rows 1 + 2 as follows:

Row 1 (RS): Sl1k, k1, repeat *k1, sl1p wyif, k3* to the end of the row.

Row 2 (WS): sl1k, k1, repeat *sl1p wyif, k1, sl1p wyif, k2* to the end of the row.

Note: See page 43 for notes on reading the charts before you begin following Chart 2.

I-CORD CAST (BIND) OFF

After completing Chart 2, ensure your last row was a WS Row. Cast off the remaining stitches using an I-cord cast off (see below) to create a neat finish at the top that matches the I-cord edges at the sides of the purse.

When casting off, knit the 2nd and 3rd stitch of each vertical slip stitch stripe together to align the slip stitch pattern.

First, place the 43 st of your provisional cast on (from Section 1) onto your right needle with the RS facing out, so that the rectangle folds in half. Don't be confused – the provisional cast on does not unravel as easily as usual due to the slipped stitches.

Slip the first 3 sts on your right needle (the 3 I-cord edge sts) back to your left needle. These will be the 3 sts for the I-cord cast off and joins your work to work the cast off in the round. Work the I-cord cast off with the RS of section 2 facing you, so you can continue working the cast off with your working yarn in the direction of a RS row. Cast off, as follows:

Step 1: K2, ssk, sl the 3 sts from your right needle back onto your left needle.

Steps 2 and 3: Repeat step 1.

Step 4: K2, sl1k, slip the next two sts together knitwise, knit all 3 slipped sts together through the back loop, sl the 3 sts from your right needle back onto your left needle.

Repeat Steps 1–4 across the remaining sts (Section 2) followed by the provisional cast on stitches (Section 1), until you have 5 sts remaining on your left needle.

Tip: To align the intarsia colour changes, change to the new colour 1 st before the colour change. This means that, when you are about to knit Step 1, there are 4 sts of the old colour on your left hand needle (1 st + 3 I-cord sts).

Repeat Step 1 a further 2 times.

To finish the I-cord cast off, use a tapestry needle and sew together the first and last 3 sts of your cast off.

JOINING THE SIDE SEAMS

Working from the RS, sew section 2 onto the 3rd I-cord st of section 1, which is at the WS of section 1 (see page 47 for visual guidance).

Step 1: Insert your needle below the loop in the middle of the 3rd I-cord st of section 1 and pull the yarn through.

Step 2: Insert your needle into the garter stitch knot of section 2 and pull your yarn through.

Repeat Steps 1 + 2 alternating to sew the side seam. For an invisible seam, change the colour of your sewing thread according to the motif.

Close the other side of the purse the same way.

FINISHING

Sew in all ends, for example by using the duplicate stitch method on the WS of your work. Gently wash your For Small Things Purse and block it according to the measurements.

ZIPPER

Sew in the zipper by hand, using a sewing thread that matches both MC and CC.

With the zipper closed, pin both ends of the zipper into the corners of the purse. Then, open the zipper and pin it in place along the sides of the purse with the I-cord edge aligned with the teeth of the zipper. To make sewing easier, you can secure the zipper by basting stitches along the opening first, so that you can remove all the pins.

Next, sew the ribbon of the zipper onto your purse by backstitching right below your I-cord cast off.

To neaten the inside of your purse, you can choose to add a cotton ribbon to hide the zipper. Start at one corner by sewing the top edge of the ribbon onto your zipper ribbon, covering the seam. When you have sewn all around the top edge, cut the end of your ribbon, leaving an about 2.5cm (1in) piece. Fold it inwards, and sew it on top of the beginning of the ribbon. Now, sew the bottom edge of the ribbon onto your purse as well.

For Small Things Purse

Note: See page 43 for notes on reading these charts before you begin following them.

CHART 2 SECTION 2

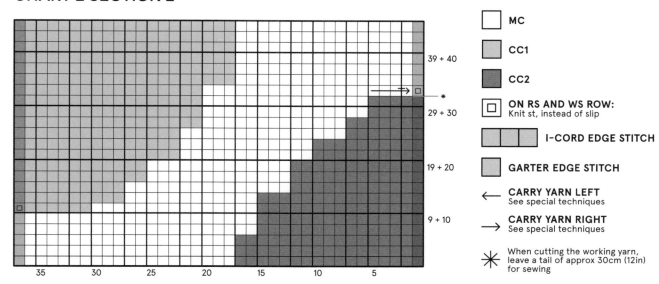

	MC
	CC1
	CC2
□	**ON RS AND WS ROW:** Knit st, instead of slip
	I-CORD EDGE STITCH
	GARTER EDGE STITCH
←	**CARRY YARN LEFT** See special techniques
→	**CARRY YARN RIGHT** See special techniques
✳	When cutting the working yarn, leave a tail of approx 30cm (12in) for sewing

CHART 1 SECTION 1

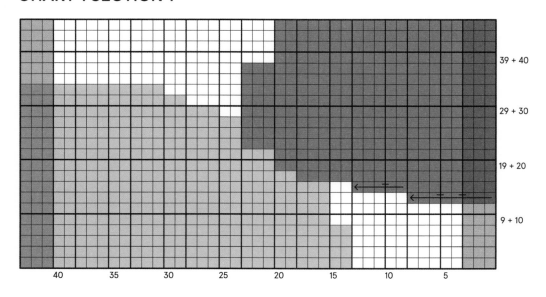

In Full Bloom Headband

The In Full Bloom Headband is another of my projects that was inspired by a day at my local botanical gardens – somewhere that always stirs my imagination. I let myself explore the place at leisure and drift aimlessly along the many winding paths and trails just taking in the beautiful shapes, colours and textures. I particularly enjoy sitting by the lake listening to the sounds of the birds while working on a knitting project or cutting out paper collages to reproduce the natural forms that have caught my eye that day, some of which are reflected in the motif for the In Full Bloom Headband. This design captures some of my favourite shapes that were created on the spot while soaking up the atmosphere.

#infullbloomheadband

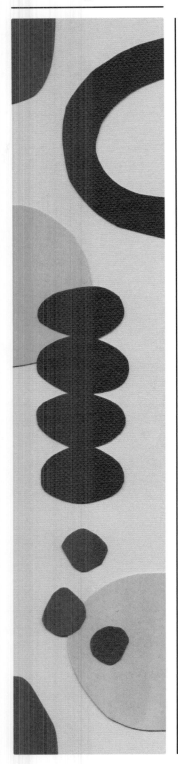

CONSTRUCTION

The In Full Bloom Headband is knitted in garter stitch in combination with the intarsia technique, which is used to create a pattern of organic shapes. It is knitted flat and sewn together at the end. An I-cord edge is worked along both edges as you knit for neat edges.

SKILL LEVEL

●●○○○

SIZES

Sizes 1 (2) 3 are designed to fit a head circumference of: 51–54 (55–58) 59–62cm / 20–21¼ (21½–22¾) 23¼–24½in. The In Full Bloom Bandana is designed to be worn with approx. 8–11cm (3¼–4¼in) negative ease. Measure your head circumference to choose a suitable size. Make sure that the measuring tape does not sit too tight or too loose, as you want your headband to fit comfortably.

FINISHED MEASUREMENTS

1. **Circumference:** 43 (47) 51cm / 17 (18½) 20in
2. **Width:** 9 (9) 9.5cm / 3½ (3½) 3¾in

YARN

4-ply (fingering weight) yarn that matches the tension (gauge) in 4 shades. As the shapes in the motif use only a small amount of yarn, this is a great project for using up leftover odds and ends in your yarn stash. You will also need waste yarn for casting on.

MC: 66 (72) 86m / 72 (79) 94yds
CC1: 24 (24) 28m / 26 (26) 31yds
CC2: 32 (32) 36m / 35 (35) 39yds
CC3: 26 (28) 34m / 29 (31) 37yds

SAMPLE 1

SAMPLE 2

Yarn used in samples: John Arbon Textiles Knit by Numbers 4ply Mini skeins (50 per cent Merino, 50 per cent Bluefaced Leicester, 100m / 109yds, 25g / ⅞oz).

Colourway for sample 1 (below, right):
MC: KBN60, 1 skein
CC1: KBN118, 1 skein
CC2: KBN45, 1 skein
CC3: KBN17, 1 skein

Colourway for sample 2 (below, left):
MC: KBN45, 1 skein
CC1: KBN17, 1 skein
CC2: KBN60, 1 skein
CC3: KBN118, 1 skein

NEEDLES
3mm (US 2.5) circular needles, or size needed to obtain the correct tension (gauge).

TENSION (GAUGE)
26 sts x 48 rows to 10 x 10cm (4 x 4in) in garter stitch, measured after washing and blocking.

READING THE CHARTS
The charts shows only RS rows. The intarsia pattern for each odd-numbered row is exactly the same for the following even-numbered row. So, for rows 1 and 2, read the chart row labelled 1 + 2 from right to left for row 1 (RS), then from left to right for row 2 (WS), and so on.

SPECIAL TECHNIQUES

INTARSIA JOIN
See pages 26–27.

I-CORD EDGE STITCH
First 3 sts of every row: K1, sl1p wyif, k1.
Last 3 sts of every row: Sl1p wyif, k1, sl1p wyif.

PATTERN

Using waste yarn, cast on **25 (25) 27 sts** using a provisional cast on method.

Set-up Row 1 (WS): Using MC, p2, k14 (14) 15, change to CC1 and k7 (7) 8, p2.

Change colours as in the previous row and work as follows:

Set-up Row 2 (RS): Kfb, k to the last 2 sts, kfb, sl1p. (2 sts increased – **27 (27) 29 sts in total**)

Set-up Row 3 (WS): K1, sl1p wyif, k1, knit to the last 3 sts, sl1p wyif, k1, sl1p wyif.

Begin working **Chart 1** (see page 54) to create the intarsia pattern and, *at the same time*, repeat **Rows 1 + 2** as follows:

Rows 1 + 2: K1, sl1p wyif, k1, knit to the last 3 sts, sl1p wyif, k1, sl1p wyif.

Note: See page 51 for notes on reading the charts before you begin following Chart 1.

After finishing Chart 1, try on your headband. Keep in mind that the garter stitch structure will grow a bit in length after washing. You can lengthen or shorten your headband by repeating or unravelling the last row of Chart 1 (ie. the last 2 rows of knitting), but be sure, you end up on a row with MC and CC1 only.

If you are happy with the length, continue as follows, changing colours as in the previous row:

Row 1 (RS): K1, sl1p wyif, k1, knit to the last 3 sts, sl1 pwise wyif, k1, sl1p wyif.

Row 2 (WS): K1, p2tog, k to the last 3 sts, p2tog, p1. (You now have 2sts decreased – **25 (25) 27 sts in total**)

Break the yarns, leaving an about 50cm (19½in) tail in each colour for binding off the seam.

CAST (BIND) OFF

Place the sts of your provisional cast on onto your right needle. Ensure that you have 16 (16) 17 sts in MC and 9 (9) 10 sts in CC1 on both of your needles.

Place both needles together so that the headband folds in half, with the WS facing towards each other and the RS facing outwards, with the last charted row on the front needle facing towards you and the cast-on stitches on the back needle facing away from you. To align the I-cord edge stitches, cast off your stitches by grafting them together as follows:

Step 1: First, insert your tapestry needle pwise into the first st on the front needle and kwise into the first stitch on the back needle, to connect both.

Step 2: On the front needle, insert your tapestry needle kwise into the first st and slip it off the needle. Go into the next st pwise. On the back needle, insert your tapestry needle pwise into the first st and slip it off the needle. Go into the next st kwise.

Step 3: On the front needle, insert your tapestry needle kwise into the first st and slip it off the needle. Go into the next st pwise. On the back needle, insert your tapestry needle kwise into the first st and slip it off the needle. Go into the next st pwise.

Repeat Step 3 until there are 3 sts remaining on each needle.

To align the intarsia colour changes, change to MC when there is 1 st of CC1 remaining on both the front and back needle.

Repeat Step 2 a further 2 times.

Repeat Step 1 once more.

FINISHING

Sew in all ends, for example by using the duplicate stitch method on the WS. Gently wash your In Full Bloom Headband and block it according to the measurements.

CHART 1

Note: See page 51 for notes on reading these charts before you begin following them.

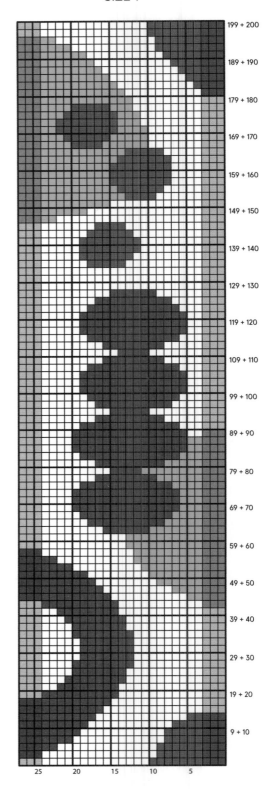

199 + 200
189 + 190
179 + 180
169 + 170
159 + 160
149 + 150
139 + 140
129 + 130
119 + 120
109 + 110
99 + 100
89 + 90
79 + 80
69 + 70
59 + 60
49 + 50
39 + 40
29 + 30
19 + 20
9 + 10

25   20   15   10   5

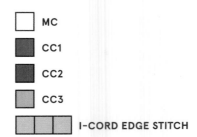

☐ MC

■ CC1

■ CC2

■ CC3

■ I-CORD EDGE STITCH

SIZE 2

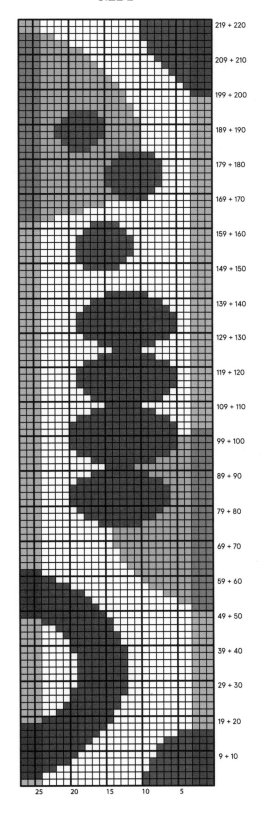

219 + 220
209 + 210
199 + 200
189 + 190
179 + 180
169 + 170
159 + 160
149 + 150
139 + 140
129 + 130
119 + 120
109 + 110
99 + 100
89 + 90
79 + 80
69 + 70
59 + 60
49 + 50
39 + 40
29 + 30
19 + 20
9 + 10

25 20 15 10 5

SIZE 3

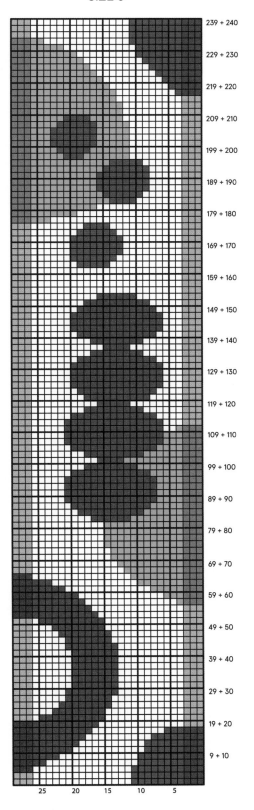

239 + 240
229 + 230
219 + 220
209 + 210
199 + 200
189 + 190
179 + 180
169 + 170
159 + 160
149 + 150
139 + 140
129 + 130
119 + 120
109 + 110
99 + 100
89 + 90
79 + 80
69 + 70
59 + 60
49 + 50
39 + 40
29 + 30
19 + 20
9 + 10

25 20 15 10 5

Looking for Treasures Tee

I am always on the lookout for interesting textures and one place I find particularly inspiring is a small island in the North Sea. At low tide, the coast stretches for kilometres. On my way from the dunes to the sea, I encounter a huge variety of natural textures – for instance, seaweed and barnacle- or algae-covered rock – that have been revealed by the retreating sea, along with multiple tiny treasures like shells and stones. While the sheerness of the fabric of the Looking For Treasures Tee conveys the lightness I feel in this place that is so special to me, the motif is inspired by the natural textures and precious found objects I collect on way to the water's edge. I like to have them represented on my tee, to keep these treasures close and remind me of the spirit of the place.

#lookingfortreasurestee

CONSTRUCTION

The Looking For Treasures Tee is a lightweight garment that plays with transparency and monochromatic shades. The tee is knitted from the top down in stocking (stockinette) stitch, using a variation of the intarsia technique, similar to marling, to create a botanical abstract motif on the front

First, you knit the back from the neckline to the point at the base where the ribbing will begin. Next, you pick up the stitches for the front and knit this side from the top down as well. The shoulder seams sit slightly towards the back, and both the front and back shoulders are shaped with short rows. After finishing the front, work the bottom ribbing all the way around the garment in the round, then do the same for the neck

ribbing. After this, you close the side seams, then pick up and knit stitches for the short sleeves, which are also worked in round. To finish the tee, add ribbing to each sleeve.

SKILL LEVEL
●●●○○

SIZES

Sizes 1 (2) 3 (4) 5 (6) 7 (8) 9 are designed to fit a bust circumference of: 76 (86) 96 (106) 116 (126) 136 (146) 156cm / 30 (34) 38 (42) 46 (50) 54 (57) 61in

The Looking For Treasures Tee is designed to be worn with approx. 16–26cm (6¼–10¼in) positive ease. Measure your bust circumference to choose a suitable size.

FINISHED MEASUREMENTS

1. Bust circumference:
97 (107) 117 (127) 137 (147) 157 (167) 177cm
/ 38¼ (42) 46 (50) 54 (57¾) 61¾ (65¾) 69¾in

2. Total length:
52 (53) 54 (55) 56 (57) 58 (59) 60cm
/ 20½ (20¾) 21¼ (21½) 22 (22½) 22¾ (23¼) 23½in

3. Length, bottom hem to armhole:
27 (27) 27 (27.3) 27.3 (27.3) 27.3 (27.3) 27.3cm
/ 10½ (10½) 10½ (10¾) 10¾ (10¾) 10¾ (10¾) 10¾in

4. Sleeve circumference:
40 (42) 44 (46) 48 (50) 52 (56) 58cm
/ 15¾ (16½) 17¼ (18) 19 (19¾) 20½ (22) 22¾in

5. Neck width:
21 (21) 22 (22) 23 (23) 24 (25) 25cm
/ 8¼ (8¼) 8½ (8½) 9 (9) 9½ (9¾) 9¾in

6. Sleeve length, from underarm:
15cm / 6in

7. Bottom, neck and sleeve ribs:
Approx. 2.3cm / 1in

Tip: If you wish to lengthen or shorten your tee, see the advice on page 12.

YARN

Work with a lace-weight mohair or an alpaca blend base yarn for the MC. For the intarsia motif, use one strand of the MC held together with one strand of 4-ply (fingering weight) yarn in a slightly lighter or darker shade to create the CC. You will also need waste yarn for casting on.

Please note, that these quantities are only estimates.
MC: 648 (720) 792 (882) 963 (1044) 1134 (1233) 1314m
/ 709 (788) 866 (965) 1054 (1142) 1241 (1349) 1347yds
CC: 135 (140) 145 (160) 165 (170) 190 (195) 200m
/ 148 (153) 159 (175) 181 (186) 208 (213) 219yds

Yarn used for the samples:
MC: Knitting For Olive, Soft Silk Mohair
(70 per cent mohair, 30 per cent silk, REACH Standard, 225m / 246yds – 25g / ⅞oz)
No. of skeins: 3 (4) 4 (5) 5 (5) 6 (6) 6
CC: Knitting For Olive, Pure Silk
(100 per cent bourette silk, 250m / 273yds – 50g / 1¾oz)
No. of skeins: 1 (1) 1 (1) 1 (1) 1 (1) 1

SAMPLE 1

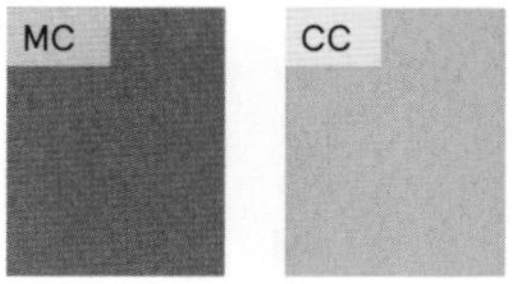

SAMPLE 2

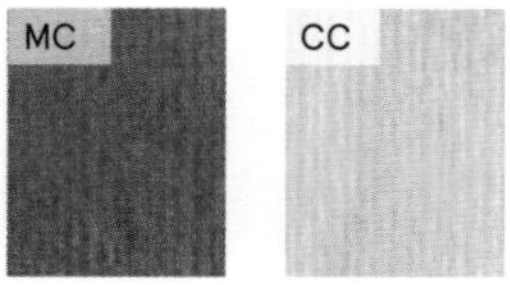

Colourway for sample 1 (shown on page 59):
MC: Dusty Robin
CC: Mandarine

Colourway for sample 2 (shown on page 60):
MC: Bottle Green
CC: Pea Shoots

NEEDLES

3.5mm (US 4) circular needles, or size needed to obtain the correct tension (gauge), for body and 3mm (US 2.5) circular needles for the ribbing.

TENSION (GAUGE)

19 sts x 34 rows to 10 x 10cm (4 x 4in) in stocking (stockinette) stitch using 3.5mm (US 4) needles and MC, measured after washing and blocking.

SPECIAL TECHNIQUES

MARLING INTARSIA VARIATION

The abstract shapes of the Looking For Treasures Tee are created using a variation of the intarsia technique to create a marled effect. To do this, one continuous strand of lightweight mohair yarn (MC) is knitted throughout the whole tee, and a 4-ply (fingering weight) yarn is added to this when knitting the motifs to give them a marled finish. For this technique, you don't need to twist your yarns as you do in regular intarsia. Instead, use several bobbins of the CC yarn to knit the different motifs.

Tip: When starting a new skein of MC, do this at the sides of the piece only. Because this tee is semi-transparent, any ends that you sew in on the WS are likely to be visible on the RS of the garment.

PATTERN

BACK

SHAPE SHOULDERS

Knit the back from the top down using a provisional cast on and shaping the shoulders by working German Short Rows.

Using 3.5mm (US 4) needles and waste yarn, cast on **90 (100) 110 (118) 126 (136) 146 (154) 164 sts** using a provisional cast on method.

Set-up Row 1 (RS): Using MC, k to the end of the row.
Set-up Row 2 (WS): P to the end of the row.

Row 1 (RS): K68 (73) 79 (83) 88 (93) 99 (105) 109 sts, turn.
Row 2 (WS): mDS, p 45 (45) 47 (47) 49 (49) 51 (55) 53 sts, turn.
Row 3 (RS): mDS, k to DS, kDS, k 3 (3) 3 (3) 3 (4) 4 (4) 4, turn.
Row 4 (WS): mDS, p to DS, pDS, p 3 (3) 3 (3) 3 (4) 4 (4) 4, turn.
Repeat Rows 3 + 4 a further 5 (7) 8 (9) 10 (9) 10 (10) 12 times.
Row 5 (RS): mDS, k to DS, kDS, k to the end of the row.
Row 6 (WS): P until DS, pDS, p to the end of the row.
Row 7 (RS): K to end of row.
Row 8 (WS): P to end of row.
Repeat Rows 7 + 8 a further 24 (24) 24 (23) 23 (25) 25 (26) 27 times, until the work measures approx. 19 (20) 20.5 (20.5) 21 (21.7) 22.3 (23.5) 24.7cm / 7½ (7¾) 8 (8) 8¼ (8½) 8¾ (9¼) 9¾in from the cast-on, measured at the centre.

ARMHOLE INCREASES

Begin working armhole increases by increasing 1 st at the beginning and end of each RS row.
Row 1 (RS): K2, M1L, k to the last 2 sts, M1R, k2. (2 sts increased)
Row 2 (WS): P to end of row.
Repeat Rows 1 + 2 a further 1 (1) 1 (1) 2 (2) 2 (2) 2 time(s). You now have **94 (104) 114 (122) 132 (142) 152 (160) 170 sts** in total.
Note: Place removable markers on both sides after finishing the armhole increases, as this will make picking up stitches for the sleeves much easier.

BODY

Row 1 (RS): K to end of row.

Row 2 (WS): P to end of row.

Repeat Rows 1 + 2 a further 41 (41) 41 (42) 42 (42) 42 (42) 42 times until work measures approx. 24.7 (24.7) 24.7 (25.3) 25.3 (25.3) 25.3 (25.3) 25.3cm / 9¾ (9¾) 9¾ (10) 10 (10) 10 (10) 10in from the armhole.

Cut the MC yarn, leaving an about 100cm (39½in) tail for sewing the side seams later.

Transfer all stitches to a stitch holder. The bottom rib will be finished in the round when both the back and the front are finished in order to align the neck and armhole ribs.

FRONT

First, each shoulder is worked separately. The German Short Rows technique is used to shape the shoulders, beginning from the neckline edge. Next, stitches are increased at the neckline to shape the front neckline, then the stitches for the shoulders are joined together in the centre to knit the front with the marled intarsia motif.

LEFT SHOULDER

Begin by unravelling the provisional cast on. Transfer the first **25 (30) 34 (38) 41 (46) 50 (53) 58 stitches** from the provisional cast on onto your working needle to knit the left shoulder, leaving **65 (70) 76 (80) 85 (90) 96 (101) 106 stitches** on a stitch holder for the neck and the right shoulder.

Start working a RS row at the neckline edge, using 3.5mm (US 4) needles and MC.

Row 1 (RS): K3 (3) 3 (3) 3 (3) 4 (3) 3, turn.

Row 2 (WS): mDS, p to the end of the row.

Row 3 (RS): K to DS, kDS, k3 (3) 3 (3) 3 (4) 4 (4) 4, turn.

Row 4 (WS): mDS, p to the end of the row.

Repeat Rows 3 + 4 a further 5 (7) 8 (9) 10 (9) 10 (10) 12 times.

Row 5 (RS): K to DS, kDS, k to the end of the row.

Row 6 (WS): P to the end of the row.

Row 7 (RS): K to the end of the row.

Row 8 (WS): P to the end of the row.

Repeat Rows 7 + 8 a further 3 (1) 0 (1) 0 (0) 0 (1) 0 time(s).

LEFT NECK INCREASES

Stitches are now increased for the neckline at the beginning of every RS row after the first 2 stitches.

Row 1 (RS): K2, M1L, k to the end of the row. (1 st increased)

Row 2 (WS): P to the end of the row.

Repeat Rows 1 + 2 a further 9 (9) 9 (9) 10 (10) 10 (11) 11 times until you have **35 (40) 44 (48) 52 (57) 61 (65) 70 sts** in total. Cut MC and transfer the sts for the left shoulder to a stitch holder.

RIGHT SHOULDER

Transfer the first **25 (30) 34 (38) 41 (46) 50 (53) 58 sts** of the provisionally cast-on sts from the stitch holder to your needle. Leave the remaining **40 (40) 42 (42) 44 (44) 46 (48) 48 sts** on the stitch holder to work the back neck later.

Start working a WS row at the neckline edge, using 3.5mm (US 4) needles and MC.

Row 1 (WS): P3 (3) 3 (3) 3 (3) 3 (4) 3, turn.

Row 2 (RS): mDS, k to the end of the row.

Row 3 (WS): P to DS, pDS, p 3 (3) 3 (3) 3 (4) 4 (4) 4, turn.

Row 4 (RS): mDS, k to the end of the row.

Repeat Rows 3 + 4 a further 5 (7) 8 (9) 10 (9) 10 (10) 12 times.

Row 5 (WS): P to DS, pDS, p to the end of the row.

Row 6 (RS): K to the end of the row.

Row 7 (WS): P to the end of the row.

Repeat Rows 6 + 7 a further 3 (1) 0 (1) 0 (0) 0 (1) 0 time(s).

RIGHT NECK INCREASES

Stitches are now increased for the neckline at the end of every RS row before the last 2 stitches.

Row 1 (RS): K to the last 2 sts, M1R, k2. (1 st increased)

Row 2 (WS): P to the end of the row.

Repeat Rows 1 + 2 a further 9 (9) 9 (9) 10 (10) 10 (11) 11 times until you have **35 (40) 44 (48) 52 (57) 61 (65) 70 sts** in total.

FRONT SECTION

Join both sets of shoulder stitches as follows:

Row 1 (RS): K to the end of the row, turn. Cast on **20 (20) 22 (22) 22 (22) 24 (24) 24 sts** using the knitted cast on method. Turn again and continue working the left shoulder stitches from the stitch holder, knitting to the end of the row. You now have **90 (100) 110 (118) 126 (136) 146 (154) 164 sts** in total.

Row 2 (WS): P to the end of the row.

Row 3 (RS): K to the end of the row.

Row 4 (WS): P to the end of the row.

Repeat Rows 3 + 4 a further 5 (6) 6 (5) 5 (6) 6 (6) 7 times, ensuring that, on the last repeat of Row 4, you place two markers within the row to indicate the beginning and the end of the stitches on which you will work the chart. Do this as follows: p21 (26) 31 (33) 37 (42) 44 (48) 53, pm, p48 (48) 48 (52) 52 (52) 58 (58) 58, pm, p21 (26) 31 (33) 37 (42) 44 (48) 53.

At this point, begin working **Chart 1** (see pages 65–67) in your chosen size to create the intarsia pattern, *ensuring you work the armhole increases on the correct chart rows, as described below.* Work the intarsia motif as follows: knit or purl (depending on whether you are on a RS or WS) using MC only to the stitch indicated in the chart, pick up CC and knit or purl using both strands for the number of stitches indicated in the chart. After finishing the motif, separate the strands, drop CC to the WS, ready for the next row, and continue knitting or purling using MC only.

To avoid the yarns from tangling, cut the CC in short tails for each shape instead of knitting from multiple skeins at the same time. For the small shapes, you will need a CC tail measuring about 1.5m (1¾yds) and, for the larger shapes, you will need a CC tail measuring about 3–6m (3¼–6½yds).

Note: For the two large hollowed out shapes, you'll need several strands of CC to avoid having floats on the WS.

Neat stitches: Each time you knit the first couple of stitches using both strands or the first stitch after changing to a single strand only, pull the yarns slightly tight, especially MC, to make sure that they mix well and to avoid having large stitches before and after each motif. Due to the change of yarn weights, some stitches might not be perfectly even, but keep in mind that when looking at the whole motif and your finished tee, it will be fine.

Weaving in ends: This technique is perfect for weaving in ends at the beginning of each shape as you knit: Add the yarn end to your working threads (3 strands in total) for about 5 sts in the next RS row.

ARMHOLE INCREASES

On **Row 33 (35) 37 (39) 39 (41) 45 (47) 49** of **Chart 1** (depending on your chosen size), begin working armhole increases by increasing 1 stitch at the beginning and the end of each RS row as follows:

Row 1 (RS): K2, M1L, k to m, sm, k according to Chart 1 to m, sm, k to the last 2 sts, M1R, k2. (2 sts increased)

Row 2 (WS): P to m, sm, p according to Chart 1 to m, sm, p to end of row.

Repeat Rows 1 + 2 a further 1 (1) 1 (1) 2 (2) 2 (2) 2 time(s) while following the chart.

You now have **94 (104) 114 (122) 132 (142) 152 (160) 170 sts** in total.

Note: Place removable markers on both sides of the front after finishing the armhole increases, as you did for the back, to make picking up stitches for the sleeves easier.

After finishing the armhole increases, continue knitting in stocking (stockinette) stitch following Chart 1.

After finishing Chart 1, continue knitting in MC in stocking stitch as follows:

Row 1 (RS): K to the end of the row, while removing markers indicating the area of stitches on which you worked the chart.

Row 2 (WS): P to the end of the row.

Repeat Rows 1 + 2 a further 11 (12) 13 (11) 12 (13) 10 (10) 11 times until the work measures approx. 24.7 (24.7) 24.7 (25.3) 25.3 (25.3) 25.3 (25.3) 25.3cm / 9¾ (9¾) 9¾ (10) 10 (10) 10 (10) 10in from the armhole.

BOTTOM RIBBING

Transfer all the back stitches from the stitch holder onto your needles so you can knit the bottom rib in the round. You will work a twisted rib, holding MC and CC together. Using 3mm (US 2.5) circular needles and MC and CC held together, work as follows:

Round 1: Repeat *k1tbl, p1* across all front sts and all back sts. Then, place a marker and join to work in the round. You now have **188 (208) 228 (244) 264 (284) 304 (320) 340 sts** in total.

Repeat Round 1 a further 8 times.

Cast (bind) off using your preferred method.

Optional: To avoid the cast off becoming too tight, for the cast off only, use a circular needle that is one size larger than the size of needle you intend to use for the ribbing. The rib might seem tight compared to the body, but it will loosen up when washed and blocked.

NECK RIBBING

Work a twisted rib at the neckline, holding MC and CC together. Begin by transferring the remaining provisionally cast-on stitches from the stitch holder onto your needles. Using 3mm (US 2.5) needles and MC and CC held together, pick up and knit stitches as follows: beginning at the left side on the back, after the held stitches from the cast on, pick up and knit 1 stitch in every other edge stitch up the side of the neckline. Then pick up and knit 1 stitch from every cast-on stitch at the front. Repeat instructions for the neckline side stitches on the right and knit all the back stitches from the provisional cast-on. When picking up stitches along the straight sides and in the cast on, insert your needle below both legs of the edge stitch and the cast on. You now have **106 (106) 110 (116) 118 (120) 124 (132) 134** sts in total.

Work the rib as follows:

Round 1: Repeat *k1tbl, p1* to the end of round.

Repeat Round 1 a further 7 times.

Cast (bind) off using your preferred method.

Optional: To avoid the cast off becoming too tight, use a larger needle size than the size of needle used to knit the ribbing.

CLOSING THE SIDE SEAMS

Close both side seams by stitching together the front and back edges using the mattress stitch.

SLEEVES

Work the sleeves in the round by picking up and knitting stitches at the shoulders.

LEFT SLEEVE

Working from the RS using 3.5mm (US 2.5) needles and MC, pick up and knit stitches beginning at the armhole edge on the front of your tee and working up along the

front, over the shoulder, then down along the back to the other armhole edge as follows: repeat *(pick up and knit in 1 edge stitch, skip 1 edge stitch) 7 (7) 6 (4) 4 (4) 3 (3) 3 times, pick up and knit in 1 edge stitch* until you have reached the end of the armhole, and eventually pick up a few extra stitches at the bottom of the armhole. You now have **76 (80) 84 (88) 92 (98) 104 (108) 114 sts** in total. Join to work in the round and place a marker at the centre of the underarm to indicate the beginning of the round.

Set-up Round: K1tbl to the end of the round.

Round 1: Knit to the end of the round.

Rounds 2–12: Repeat Round 1.

Round 13: K2tog, knit to the last 2 sts, ssk. (2 sts decreased)

Repeat Rounds 1–13 a further 2 times.

Work Round 1 a further 3 times.

You now have **70 (74) 78 (82) 86 (92) 98 (102) 108 sts** in total.

Work a twisted rib at the bottom of the sleeve, holding MC and CC together. Using 3mm (US 2.5) circular needles and MC and CC held together, work as follows:

Round 1: Repeat *k1tbl, p1* to the end of round.

Repeat Round 1 a further 7 times.

Cast (bind) off using your preferred method, for example the standard cast off or a sewn cast off.

Optional: To avoid the cast off becoming too tight, use a larger needle size than the size of needle used to knit the ribbing.

RIGHT SLEEVE

Work as for the left sleeve. To pick up stitches, working from the RS, begin at the armhole edge on the back of your tee and work up along the back, over the shoulder, then down along the front to the other armhole edge.

FINISHING

Sew in all remaining ends using the duplicate stitch method on the WS.

Gently wash your Looking For Treasures Tee and block it according to the measurements of your chosen size.

CHART 1

Note: See page 13 for notes on reading these charts before you begin following them.

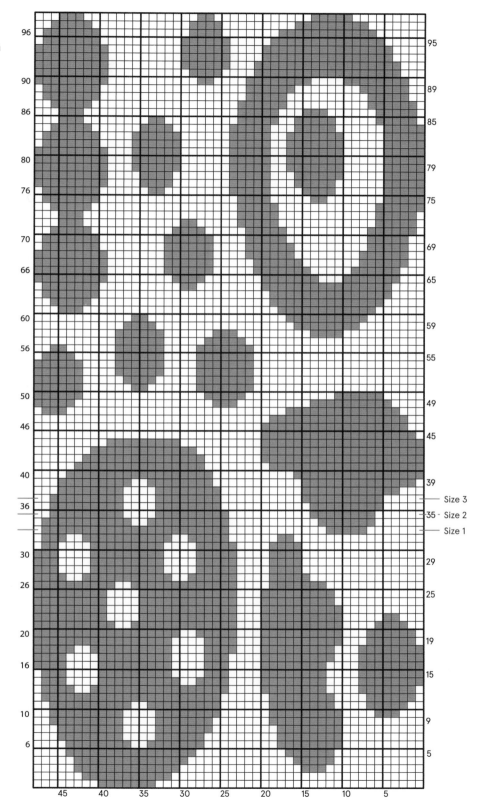

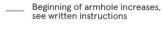
MC

CC

—— Beginning of armhole increases, see written instructions

CHART 1

See page 65 for key.

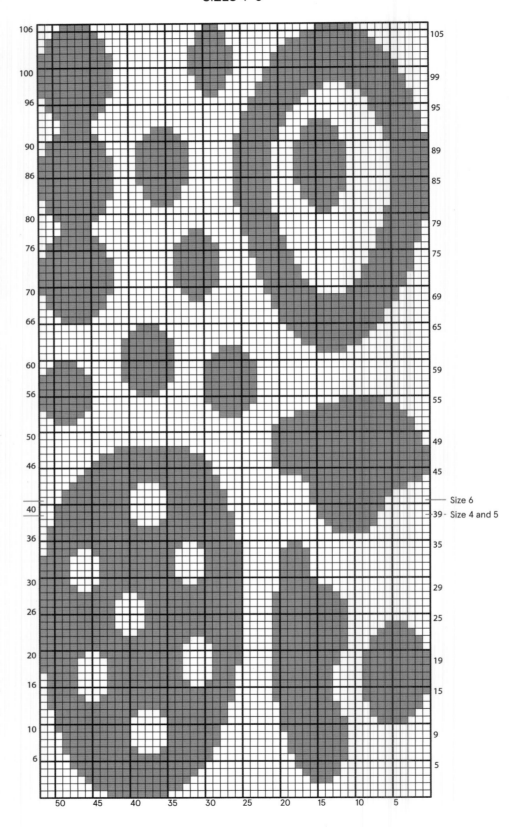

Size 6
Size 4 and 5

CHART 1

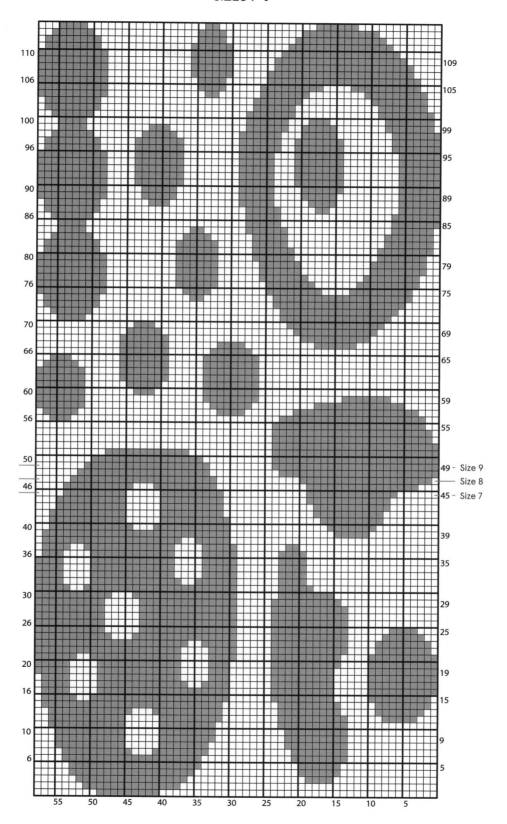

Looking for Treasures Tee

All Day at the Beach Bag

The All Day At The Beach Bag is inspired by dreamy days spent by the sea, with the warmth of the sun on my face on walks along the beach while looking for pieces of amber and other special stones and shells to collect. I love taking a break from everyday life to slow down and read a book. Listening to the sound of the breaking waves while knitting a fun summer project is one of my favourite things to do.

#alldayatthebeachbag

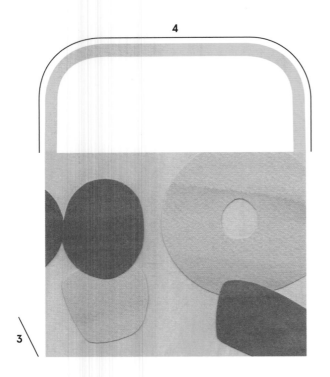

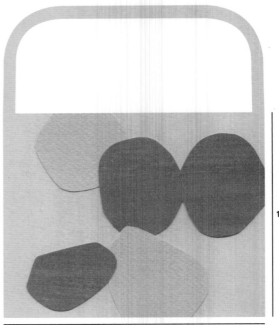

CONSTRUCTION

The All Day At The Beach Bag is worked flat in a slip stitch textural pattern, which creates three-dimensional textured stripes as well as a firm fabric that is suitable for bags. The intarsia technique is also used, creating a bold botanical motif using three colours.

The front and back of the bag are made by knitting two large rectangular panels, each worked with a garter stitch edge stitch at both sides, and finished by working an I-cord cast (bind) off along the top edge. Next, two long, thin rectangles are knitted, each with an I-cord edge stitch at the sides for neat edges. The second rectangle is joined to the first by picking up stitches from the cast-on edge of the first rectangle, then knitting in the opposite direction. The two joined pieces create a long, thin strip that forms the gusset of the bag as well as the strap.

SKILL LEVEL

●●●●○

FINISHED MEASUREMENTS

1. **Height**: 33cm (13in)
2. **Width**: 43cm (17in)
3. **Depth**: 8cm (3¼in)
4. **Length of the straps, measured from I-cord cast (bind) off**: 53cm (21in)

YARN

Heavy weight DK or lightweight aran (worsted weight) yarn in a blend of wool and plant fibres for strength.

MC: 412m (451yds)
CC1: 168m (184yds)
CC2: 170m (186yds)

Yarn used in the sample: De Rerum Natura Robinson (70 per cent Organic merino d'Arles (France) and 30 per cent recycled cotton, including 2 per cent of other recycled fibres, 250m / 273yds – 100g / 3½oz)
MC: pêche melba, 2 skeins
CC1: grand bleu, 1 skein
CC2: azur, 1 skein

NEEDLES
3.75mm (US 5) circular needles or size needed to obtain the correct tension (gauge).

TENSION (GAUGE)
26 sts x 46 rows equal 10 x 10cm (4 x 4in) in the slip stitch pattern, measured after washing and blocking.

Knit a swatch in the slip stitch pattern to determine which needle size you need to achieve the correct tension. For the tension swatch, work the slip stitch pattern as follows: Cast on a multiple of 5 sts plus 2 sts, using the long-tail cast on method.
Set-up Row (WS): Repeat *k2, sl1p wyif, k1, sl1p wyif* to the last 2 sts, k2.
Row 1 (RS): Sl1k, k1, repeat *k1, sl1p wyif, k3* to the end of the row.
Row 2 (WS): Sl1k, k1, repeat *sl1p wyif, k1, sl1p wyif, k2* to the end of the row.
Repeat Rows 1 + 2 until your swatch is big enough for checking the gauge.

Note: Stitches are counted from the RS, counting 3 stitches for each slip stitch stripe as well as 2 rows for each garter stitch ridge.

READING THE CHARTS
The charts show only RS rows. The intarsia pattern for each odd-numbered row is exactly the same for the following even-numbered row. So, for rows 1 and 2, read the chart row labelled 1 + 2 from right to left for row 1 (RS), then from left to right for row 2 (WS), and so on.

SPECIAL TECHNIQUES

INTARSIA JOIN
See pages 26–27.

CARRYING YARNS AND BINDING FLOATS
See pages 28–29.

INTARSIA CAST ON USING MULTIPLE COLOURS
See page 30.

SLIP STITCH PATTERN
The slip stitch pattern combines a garter stitch background with vertical lines in slipped sts. Each vertical stripe consists of 3 stitches. On a RS row, the second stitch is slipped and, on a WS row, the first and third stitches are slipped, which pushes the 3 stitches together into a protruding vertical stripe.

GARTER STITCH EDGE STITCH
First st of every row: Sl1k
Last st of every row: K1.

I-CORD EDGE STITCH
First 3 sts of every row: K1, sl1p wyif, k1.
Last 3 sts of every row: Sl1p wyif, k1, sl1p wyif.

PATTERN

FRONT PANEL
The shapes of motifs on the front (and the back) appear to extend beyond the edges of the rectangles, which means you need to cast on using multiple colours (see page 30). Using the long-tail cast-on method, cast on as follows: using CC1, cast on **25 sts**, using MC, cast on **87 sts**. You now have **112 sts in total**.
Set-up Row (WS): Repeat *k2, sl1p wyif, k1, sl1p wyif* to the last 2 sts, k2, changing colours as per the cast on.

Begin working **Chart 1** (see page 77) to create the intarsia colour pattern while, *at the same time*, creating the slip stitch textural pattern by repeating **Rows 1 + 2** as follows:
Row 1 (RS): Sl1k, k1, repeat *k1, sl1p wyif, k3* to the end of the row.
Row 2 (WS): Sl1k, k1, repeat *sl1p wyif, k1, sl1p wyif, k2* to the end of the row.
Note: See left for notes on reading the charts before you begin following Chart 1.

I-CORD CAST (BIND) OFF
After completing Chart 1, cast off the sts using an I-cord cast off to create a neat finish at the top that matches the I-cord edge stitches at the sides of the bag.

When casting off, knit the 2nd and 3rd stitch of each vertical slip stitch stripe together to align the slip stitch pattern.

Using MC, cast on **3 sts** using the knitted cast on method. This will be the 3 sts for your I-cord cast (bind) off. Cast off as follows:

Step 1: K2, ssk, sl the 3 sts from your right hand needle back onto your left hand needle. Repeat Step 1 a further 2 times.

Step 2: K2, sl1k, slip the next 2 sts together knitwise, knit all 3 slipped sts together through the back loop. Sl the 3 sts of your right needle back onto your left needle.

Repeat *Work Step 1 three times, work Step 2 one time* until you have 5 sts remaining on your left needle, including your three I-cord stitches while, *at the same time*, changing colours according to the motif as instructed below.

To align the intarsia colour changes, change to the new colour 1 st before the colour change. This means that, when you are about to knit Step 1, there are 4 sts of the old colour on your left hand needle (1 st + three I-cord sts), and when you are about to knit Step 2, there are 5 sts left on your left hand needle (1 st + 1 decrease st + three I-cord sts).

Repeat Step 1 a further 2 times.
Cast off the remaining 3 sts on your left needle as follows: K1, k2tog, cast off one stitch.

Cut MC and continue with the back.

BACK PANEL
As for the front, you need to cast on using multiple colours for the back. Using the long-tail cast-on method, cast on as follows: using MC, cast on **25 sts**, using CC2, cast on **30 sts**, using MC, cast on **57 sts**. You now have **112 sts** in total.

Complete the back by following the instructions for the front, but following Chart 2 (see page 78) to create the intarsia colour pattern.

BAG GUSSET AND STRAP
The gusset of the bag that runs across the base and up the sides extends up beyond the sides of the bag to create the strap. It is formed by two long, thin knitted rectangles that are joined together at the part of the gusset that sits at the centre of the base of the bag. This gusset is sewn to the front and back panels to join them together in a box shape. The rectangles are knitted in the slip stitch pattern, working an I-cord edge stitch along both sides as you knit.

RECTANGLE 1
Using MC and the long-tail cast-on method, cast on **23 sts**, leaving a tail of approx. 30cm (12in) for sewing later.

Set-up Row (WS): K1, sl1p wyif, k1, repeat *k2, sl1p wyif, k1, sl1p wyif* to the end of the row.

Begin working **Chart 3** (see page 79) to create the intarsia colour pattern, following the charted instructions to leave tails of yarn for sewing together while, *at the same time*, creating the slip stitch textural pattern by repeating Rows 1 + 2 as follows:

Row 1 (RS): Repeat *k1, sl1p wyif, k3* until the last 3 sts, sl1p wyif, k1, sl1p wyif.
Row 2 (WS): K1, sl1p wyif, k1, repeat *k2, sl1p wyif, k1, sl1p wyif* to the end of the row.
Note: See page 71 for notes on reading the charts before you begin following Chart 3.

After finishing **Row 90 of Chart 3**, place a removable marker on both ends of the row, to mark the end of the base. Do the same after **Row 238 of Chart 3**, to mark the the top corner of the bag – the point at which the strap section of the rectangle begins.

Strap: After finishing Chart 3, continue with MC only to knit the strap section, working the slip stitch pattern as follows:
Row 1 (RS): Repeat *k1, sl1p wyif, k3* to the last 3 sts, sl1p wyif, k1, sl1p wyif.
Row 2 (WS): K1, sl1p wyif, k1, repeat *k2, sl1p wyif, k1, sl1p wyif* to the end of the row.
Repeat **Rows 1 + 2** a further 49 times or until the strap has your preferred length.
Place the sts on a stitch holder.

RECTANGLE 2
Like Rectangle 1, Rectangle 2 is knitted from the bottom up, this time starting at the cast-on edge of Rectangle 1 – you pick up and knit stitches from the cast-on edge

of Rectangle 1 and knit in the opposite direction to knit Rectangle 2, after which you have a long strip to use as the bag gusset.

Using MC and leaving a tail of approx. 60cm (23½in) for sewing the side seam later, pick up and knit **23 sts** from the cast-on edge of Rectangle 1 by inserting your needle below both legs of each cast-on st to pick up a new st.

Set-up Row (WS): K1, sl1p wyif, k1, repeat *k2, sl1p wyif, k1, sl1p wyif* to the end of the row.

Begin working **Chart 4** (see page 79) to create the intarsia colour pattern, following the charted instructions to leave tails of yarn for sewing together while, *at the same time*, creating the slip stitch textural pattern by repeating **Rows 1 + 2** as as given under Rectangle 1.
Again, after finishing **Row 90** and **Row 238** of **Chart 4,** place a removable marker at both ends of the rows.

Strap: After finishing **Chart 4**, follow the instructions under Rectangle 1 for knitting the strap section.

You now have one long rectangular piece for the gusset of the bag.

JOINING ALL PIECES TOGETHER

First of all, sew in all ends that are not needed for sewing your All Day At The Beach Bag using, for example, the duplicate stitch method. Gently wash all 3 pieces and block them according to the measurements.

Note that Rectangle 1 joins the left side of the front to the right side of the back. Rectangle 2 joins the right side of the front to the left side of the back. The intarsia pattern for each rectangle aligns with the intarsia patterns on both the front and back panels – see the letters A to E on the charts to guide you when joining the pieces so that the intarsia patterns align.

Sew the front and back panels onto the I-cord edge sts of the gusset, starting with the front panel. First, pin everything in place: the markers on the base section of the gusset need to align with the first and the last stitch of the cast-on edges of the front and back panels, and the upper markers on the gusset need to align with the upper edges of the front and the back panels, just below the I-cord cast (bind) off.

Working from the RS, sew the cast-on edge of the front panel onto the WS of the 3rd I-cord stitch of the gusset, which is at the WS. Work with the visible sts of the front only (ie. the 2 knit sts alternating with 2 garter sts of the textural pattern). Starting at the centre of the gusset (where the two rectangles meet), work as follows:

1 and 3.

2.

4.

Step 1: Insert your needle below the loop in the middle of the 3rd I-cord stitch of the gusset and pull the yarn through.

Step 2: Insert your needle under both legs of the st in the first row of the front panel, after the cast-on edge.

Repeat Steps 1 + 2 to sew the bottom seam. For an invisible seam, change the colour of your sewing thread according to the motif.

When you reach the last st of the front cast-on edge, skip 1 I-cord edge st of the gusset (which is 1 st before the marker) to create a more precise corner.

Step 3: Insert your needle below the loop in the middle of the 3rd I-cord stitch of the gusset and pull the yarn through.

Step 4: Insert your needle into the garter stitch knot of the front panel and pull your yarn through.

Repeat Steps 3 + 4 to sew the side seam, again changing the colour of your sewing thread according to the motif for an invisible seam.

When you've reached the I-cord cast (bind) off of the front panel, insert your needle below both legs of the I-cord sts to secure it to the gusset.

After finishing one half of the front seam, begin again at the centre of the base to finish the other half of the front. Remember to skip 1 I-cord edge st of the gusset at the corner, before you continue sewing the side seam.

When you've finished attaching the gusset to the front panel, repeat the process to attach the other edge of the gusset to the back panel.

COMPLETING THE STRAP

Pin both ends of the strap together to check you are happy with the length. You can unravel a few rows or add repeats of **Rows 1 + 2** of the strap instructions to make the strap shorter or longer. If you are happy with the result, finish the straps as follows:

Return your stitches from hold onto separate needles and work the following row on both straps:

Row 1 (RS): K1, k2tog, repeat *k3, k2tog* to the last 5 sts, k2, k2tog, k1.

Align both needles with the WS facing each other and the RS facing you and bind off your stitches by grafting them together as follows:

Step 1: On the front needle, insert your tapestry needle kwise into the first st and slip it off the needle. Go into the next st pwise. On the back needle, insert your tapestry needle pwise into the first st and slip it off the needle. Go into the next st kwise.

Step 2: On the front needle, insert your tapestry needle kwise into the first st and slip it off the needle. Go into the next st pwise. On the back needle, insert your tapestry needle kwise into the first st and slip it off the needle. Go into the next st pwise.

Step 3: Repeat Step 2.

Step 4: Repeat Step 1.

Repeat Steps 1–4 a further 3 times.

Repeat Step 1 one more time. Go into the last st of the front needle kwise and slip it off, go into the last stitch of the back needle pwise and slip that st off the needle.

FINISHING

Sew in the remaining ends.

CHART 1
FRONT PANEL

Note: See page 71 for notes on reading these charts before you begin following them.

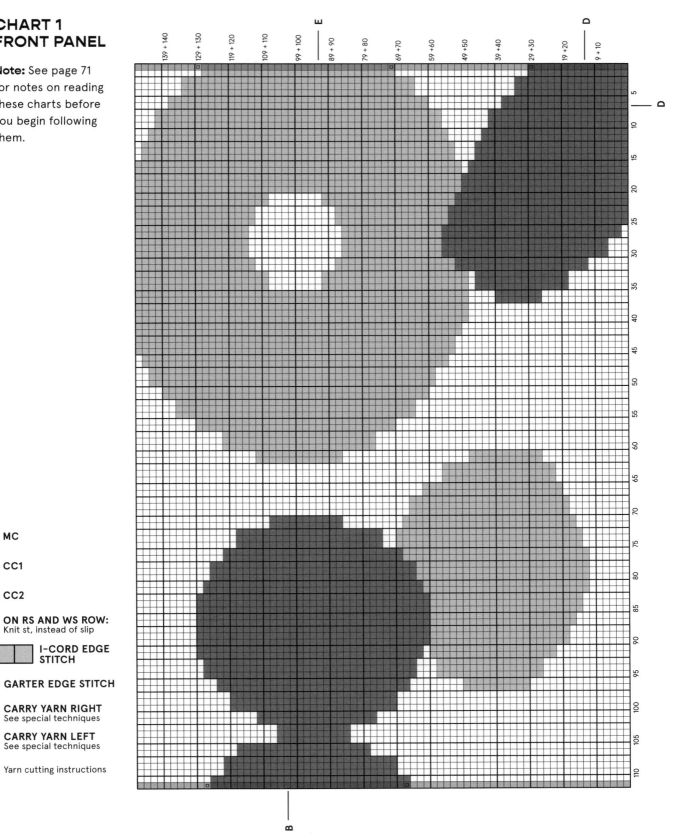

MC

CC1

CC2

ON RS AND WS ROW:
Knit st, instead of slip

I-CORD EDGE STITCH

GARTER EDGE STITCH

→ **CARRY YARN RIGHT**
See special techniques

← **CARRY YARN LEFT**
See special techniques

✳ Yarn cutting instructions

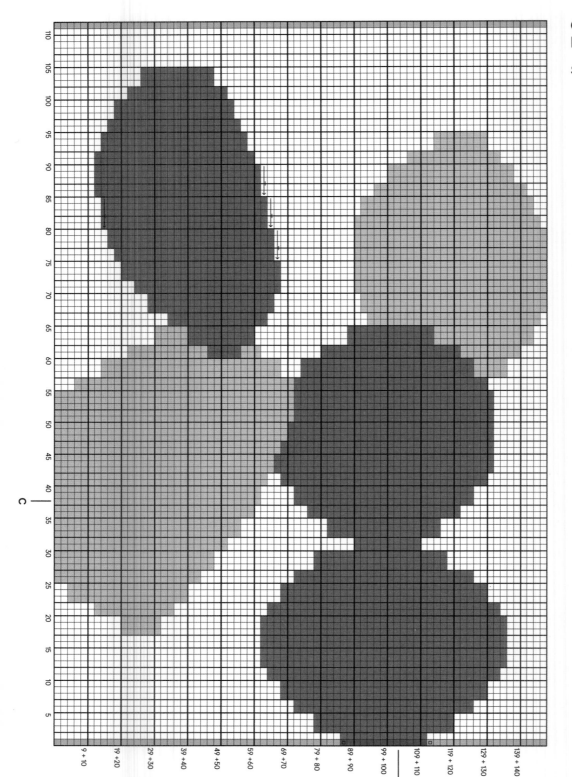

CHART 2
BACK PANEL

See page 77 for key

CHART 3
RECTANGLE 1

CHART 4
RECTANGLE 2

* **1** When cutting the working yarn, leave a tail of approx. 30cm (12in) for sewing

* **2** When beginning with the new yarn, leave a tail of approx. 30cm (12in) for sewing

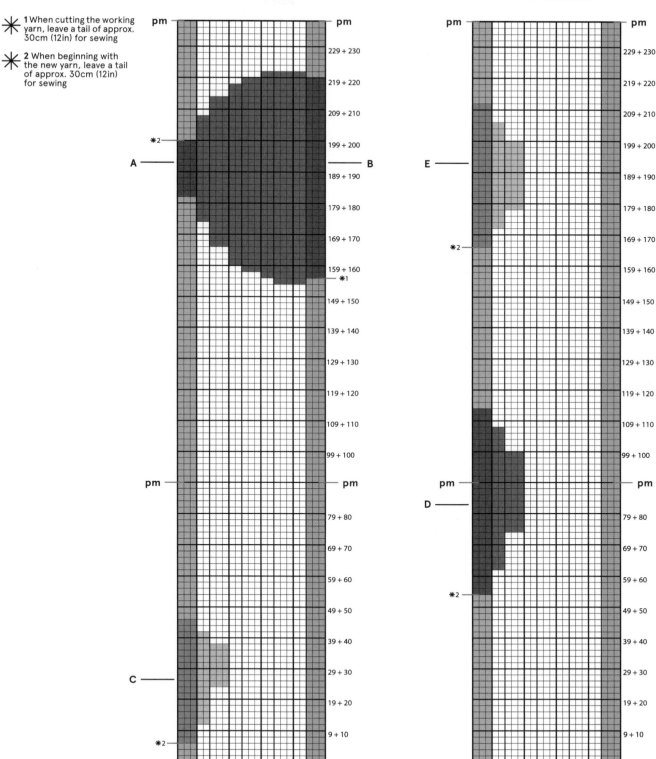

Along the Coast Vest

There is a special place on an island in the North Sea, one of the northernmost places in my home country, which inspires the abstract pattern of the Along the Coast Vest. You approach the shore via a narrow path between the dunes and, all of a sudden, a breathtaking view opens out in front of you! Beyond the dunes, with their unique textures and colours, and the narrow strip of shoreline, the Wadden Sea stretches out to the horizon. Standing in that spot, I look to the left, then to the right – and it is precisely these views that are represented by the intarsia motifs on the front and back of this vest. The sea is smooth and it is very quiet there, so I take some time to sit down to watch the sea birds and enjoy the peace and tranquillity.

#alongthecoastvest

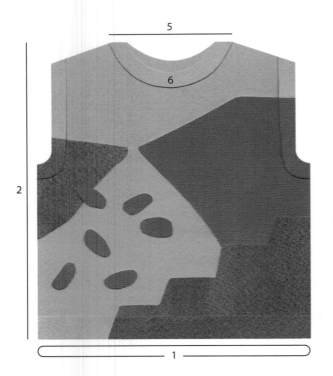

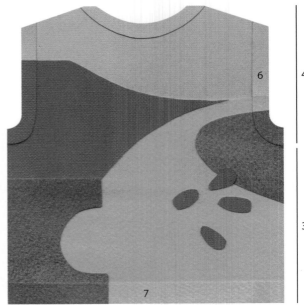

CONSTRUCTION

The Along The Coast Vest is knitted from the top down in brioche stitch, using the intarsia technique to create an abstract pattern of a landscape by the sea. One continuous main colour is knitted throughout the whole vest, while the contrasting colours change according to the intarsia colour chart.

First, you knit the back from the neckline to the point at the base where the ribbing will begin. Next, stitches for the front are picked up at the shoulders and you knit this side from the top down as well. The shoulder seam sits slightly towards the back. After finishing the front, the ribbing around the bottom and the armholes are added using the seamless intarsia technique in the round, to allow the motif to continue into the ribs as well. Finally, the side seams are closed and a folded neck rib is knitted to complete your Along The Coast Vest.

SKILL LEVEL
●●●●●

SIZES

Sizes 1 (2) 3 (4) 5 (6) 7 (8) 9 are designed to fit a bust circumference of:
76 (86) 96 (106) 116 (126) 136 (146) 156cm
/ 30 (34) 38 (42) 46 (50) 54 (57) 61in

The Along The Coast Vest is designed to be worn with approx. 12–22cm (4¾–8¾in) positive ease. Measure your bust circumference to choose a suitable size.

FINISHED MEASUREMENTS

1. Bust circumference:
93 (103) 113 (123) 133 (143) 153 (163) 173cm
/ 36½ (40½) 44½ (48½) 52¼ (56¼) 60¼ (64¼) 68in

2. Total length:
51 (52) 53 (54) 55 (56) 57 (58) 59cm
/ 20 (20½) 21 (21¼) 21¾ (22) 22½ (22¾) 23¼in

3. Length, bottom hem to armhole:
27 (27) 28 (27) 28 (29) 29 (29) 29cm
/ 10½ (10½) 11 (10½) 11 (11½) 11½ (11½) 11½in

4. Armhole depth:
24 (25) 25 (27) 27 (27) 28 (29) 30cm
/ 9½ (9¾) 9¾ (10½) 10½ (10½) 11 (11½) 11¾in

5. Neck width:
16.5 (16.5) 16.5 (19) 19 (19) 22.5 (22.5) 22.5cm
/ 6½ (6½) 6½ (7½) 7½ (7½) 8¾ (8¾) 8¾in
6. Neck and armhole rib: Approx. 3cm / 1¼in
7. Bottom rib: Approx. 4.5cm / 1¾in

YARN
Work with an aran (worsted) weight yarn in
5 different shades.

Note that these quantities are only estimates.
MC: 266 (306) 360 (373) 410 (450) 504 (531) 563m
/ 291 (335) 394 (408) 449 (492) 551 (581) 616yds
CC1: 108 (126) 153 (162) 167 (184) 202 (216) 229m
/ 118 (138) 167 (177) 183 (201) 221 (236) 250yds
CC2: 74 (90) 92 (103) 113 (124) 135 (146) 155m
/ 81 (98) 100 (112) 124 (136) 148 (160) 169yds
CC3: 113 (144) 153 (158) 175 (193) 209 (225) 239m
/ (124 (158) 167 (173) 191 (211) 228 (246) 262yds
CC4: 124 (140) 158 (175) 193 (216) 230 (248) 265m
/ 136 (154) 173 (191) 211 (236) 252 (272) 290yds

Yarn used in the sample:
Järbo Svensk Ull 3 tr (100 per cent Swedish wool,
180m / 197yds – 100g / 3½oz)

Colourway for sample 1 (shown on page 81):
MC: Bauer Forest (59019), 2 (2) 3 (3) 3 (3) 3 (3) 4 skeins
CC1: April Sun (59005), 1 (1) 1 (1) 2 (2) 2 (2) 2 skein(s)
CC2: Copper Mine (59016), 1 (1) 1 (1) 1 (1) 1 (1) 1 skein
CC3: Rhubarb Lemonade (59006), 1 (1) 1 (1) 1 (2) 2 (2) 2
skein(s)
CC4: Midsummer Green (59014), 1 (1) 1 (2) 2 (2) 2 (2) 2
skein(s)

Colourway for sample 2 (shown on page 81):
MC: Bergslagen Dark Blue (59015)
CC1: Rhubarb Lemonade (59006)
CC2: Plum Harvest (59010)
CC3: Dala Blue (59012)
CC4: Copper Mine (59016)

NEEDLES
3.5mm (US 4) circular needles, or size needed to obtain
correct tension (gauge) for the brioche stitch, 3mm
(US 2.5) circular needles for the ribbing, and 4.5mm
(US 7) needles for casting on.

SAMPLE 1

| MC | CC1 | CC2 | CC3 | CC4 |

SAMPLE 2

| MC | CC1 | CC2 | CC3 | CC4 |

TENSION (GAUGE)
16.5 sts x 46 rows (23 brioche rows counting from RS) to
10 x 10cm (4 x 4in) in brioche stitch, measured after
washing and blocking. Knit a swatch in brioche stitch to
determine which needle size you need to achieve the
correct tension. Note that, with brioche stitch, it is
particularly important to block your tension swatch, as
the stitches grow a lot after washing.

As the Along The Coast Vest uses a two-colour brioche
techniqe, it's recommended that you feel comfortable
knitting one-colour brioche stitch before you begin
knitting the vest. The main difference with two-colour
brioche compared to one-colour, is that you knit each
row twice. First, knit the RS row in CC, then slide the work
back across your circular needle to knit the same RS row
again using MC. After these two rows you turn your work
to knit the WS row twice as well, again, first with the CC,
then with the MC.

For the tension swatch, work the brioche stitch as follows.
Cast on an odd number of sts using the long-tail
cast-on method.
Set-up Row CC (WS): Using CC, k1, repeat *p1, sl1yo* to
the last 2 sts, p1, sl1p wyif. *Do not turn, instead slide the
work back across your circular needle to work this WS
row again.*
Set-up Row MC (WS): Using MC, k1, repeat *sl1yo, brk* to
the last 2 sts, sl1yo, sl1p wyif. Turn work.
Row 1 CC (RS): K1, repeat *brk, sl1yo* until the last 2 sts,
brk, sl1p wyif. *Do not turn, instead slide the work back
across your circular needle to work this RS row again
as Row 2. This instruction will be indicated as "Do not
turn, slide".*

Row 2 MC (RS): K1, repeat *sl1yo, brp* until the last 2 sts, sl1yo, sl1p wyif. Turn work.

Row 3 CC (WS): K1, repeat *brp, sl1yo* until the last 2 sts, brp, sl1p wyif. *Do not turn, slide.*

Row 4 MC (WS): K1, repeat *sl1yo, brk* until the last 2 sts, sl1yo, sl1p wyif. Turn work.

Repeat Rows 1–4 until your swatch is large enough to check the tension.

SPECIAL TECHNIQUES

INTARSIA JOIN
See pages 26–27.

EDGE STITCH
Create an edge by alternating one MC stitch and one CC stitch repeatedly.
First stitch of every row: K1.
Last stitch of every row: Sl1p wyif.

PATTERN

BACK
Knit the back from the top down. To avoid the cast on becoming too tight, cast on using a larger needle size than your main knitting needles, and change to your main needles after the cast-on row. Using 4.5mm (US 7) needles and CC1, cast on **57 (65) 73 (77) 85 (93) 99 (107) 115 sts** using the long-tail cast-on method. Change to 3.5mm (US 4) needles and turn.

Set-up Row CC (WS): K1, repeat *p1, sl1yo* to the last 2 sts, p1, sl1p wyif. *Do not turn, slide.*

Set-up Row MC (WS): K1, repeat *sl1yo, brk* to the last 2 sts, sl1yo, sl1p wyif. Turn work.

Row 1 CC (RS): K1, repeat *brk, sl1yo* to the last 2 sts, brk, sl1p wyif. *Do not turn, slide.*

Row 2 MC (RS): K1, repeat *sl1yo, brp* to the last 2 sts, sl1yo, sl1p wyif. Turn work.

Row 3 CC (WS): K1, repeat *brp, sl1yo* to the last 2 sts, brp, sl1p wyif. *Do not turn, slide.*

Row 4 MC (WS): K1, repeat *sl1yo, brk* to the last 2 sts, sl1yo, sl1p wyif. Turn work.

Repeat Rows 1–4 a further 7 (7) 8 (7) 7 (7) 8 (8) 8 times, until you have 17 (17) 19 (17) 17 (17) 19 (19) 19 brioche rows in CC1.

CHART 1
Begin working **Chart 1** (see pages 94 + 96 + 98) in your chosen size while, at the same time, working in brioche stitch by repeating Rows 1–4 above. Please note that armhole increases are not indicated in the charts. Follow the written instructions (see below, under Armhole Increases) alongside the chart.

Note: The charts show only CC rows. Add a MC row after every CC row. Narrow boxes indicate sts worked in MC, while wider boxes represent sts worked in CC yarns.

Intarsia joins: As it is not that obvious where to change colours when knitting brioche intarsia, there are black outlines around each motif marking the position of the intarsia joins. In CC RS rows always change colours after the sl1yo; in CC WS rows change colours after the brp.

Tip: If the pattern changes more than 3 brioche stitches, it is recommended to either cut the yarn and start again with a new ball, or carry the yarn to the left or to the right (see pages 28–29) to prevent the float on the WS becoming too long.

Motif: As the motifs of the back and front have the same amount of rows, you could easily flip both motifs, if you prefer, by knitting Chart 2 for the back and Chart 1 for the front.

ARMHOLE INCREASES
On **Row 27 (29) 29 (29) 29 (29) 29 (31) 33 of Chart 1,** begin working armhole increases by increasing 2 sts at the beginning and the end of each RS row worked in CC (row 1 of the brioche 4-row sequence) and, *at the same time,* change colours as indicated in the chart:

4 st Increase Row CC (RS): K1, brk, sl1yo, brkyobrk, sl1yo, repeat *brk, sl1yo* to the last 4 sts, brkyobrk, sl1yo, brk, sl1p wyif. *Do not turn, slide.* (4 sts increased)

4 st Increase Row MC (RS): K1, sl1yo, brp, sl1yo, p1, repeat *sl1yo, brp* to the last 6 sts, sl1yo, p1, sl1yo, brp, sl1yo, sl1p wyif. Turn work.

On **Row 35 (37) 37 (39) 39 (39) 41 (43) 45 of Chart 1,** increase 3 sts at the beginning and the end of the RS row in CC and, *at the same time,* change colours as indicated in the chart:

6 st Increase Row CC (RS): Kfb, brk, sl1yo, brkyobrk, sl1yo, repeat *brk, sl1yo* until the last 4 sts, brkyobrk, sl1yo, brk, kfb. *Do not turn, slide.* (6 sts increased)

6 st Increase Row MC (RS): K1, p1, sl1yo, brp, sl1yo, p1, repeat *sl1yo, brp* until the last 7 sts, sl1yo, p1, sl1yo, brp, sl1yo, p1, sl1p wyif. Turn work. You now have 79 (87) 95 (103) 111 (119) 129 (137) 145 sts in total.

BODY

After finishing the armhole increases, there is a slight change in the pattern. Continue knitting **Chart 1** to create the intarsia pattern and, *at the same time*, repeat **Rows 1–4** as follows:

Note: After the 6 st armhole increase you begin with Row 3.

Row 1 CC (RS): K1, repeat *sl1yo, brk* to the last 2 sts, sl1yo, sl1p wyif. *Do not turn, slide.*

Row 2 MC (RS): K1, repeat *brp, sl1yo* to the last 2 sts, brp, sl1p wyif. Turn work.

Row 3 CC (WS): K1, repeat *sl1yo, brp* to the last 2 sts, sl1yo, sl1p wyif. *Do not turn, slide.*

Row 4 MC (WS): K1, repeat *brk, sl1yo* to the last 2 sts, brk, sl1p wyif. Turn work.

After finishing Chart 1 in your chosen size, break MC, leaving a tail of approx. 60–80cm (23½–31½in) for sewing the side seam later. To avoid the rib becoming too tight, you now increase 2 sts in every 4th brioche stitch for the bottom rib in CC only.

Changing colours as in the previous row, knit the next row as follows:

Row 1 CC (RS): K1, sl1yo, repeat *(brk, sl1yo) 3 times, **brkyobrk**, sl1yo* until the last 5 (5) 5 (5) 5 (5) 7 (7) 7 sts, repeat *brk, sl1yo* 2 (2) 2 (2) 2 (2) 3 (3) 3 times, sl1p wyif. *Turn work.*

Row 2 CC (WS): K2tog (the first st together with the brioche st), p1, repeat *brk, p1* 2 (2) 2 (2) 2 (2) 3 (3) 3 times in total, work *k1, p1, (brk, p1) 4 times* until the end of the row. Remember to change colours as in the previous row. You now have **96 (106) 116 (126) 136 (146) 158 (168) 178 sts** in total.

Break the yarns and place all sts on a stitch holder. The bottom rib will be finished in the round when both the back and the front are finished, to align the neck and armhole ribs.

FRONT

LEFT SHOULDER

First, each shoulder is worked separately, increasing at the neckline to shape it. Then, these stitches are joined together to knit the front with the intarsia motif. Starting with the left shoulder, stitches are picked up according to the brioche ribs at the back, which means you pick up and knit 1 st in MC followed by 1 st in CC1. When picking up stitches, insert your needle into the stitch below both legs of the cast on.

With the RS facing you, count 15 (19) 23 (23) 27 (31) 31 (35) 39 sts in from the left edge. This marks where you begin picking up sts for the front shoulder. Using 3.5mm (US 4) needles, repeat *using MC pick up and knit 1, using CC1 pick up and knit 1* until the last st. Using CC1, pick up and knit the last st as well: You now have **15 (19) 23 (23) 27 (31) 31 (35) 39 sts** in total.

Set-up Row CC (WS): K1, repeat *p1, sl1yo* to the last 2 sts, p1, sl1p wyif. *Do not turn, slide.*

Set-up Row MC (WS): K1, repeat *sl1yo, brk* to the last 2 sts, sl1yo, sl1p wyif. Turn work.

Row 1 CC (RS): K1, repeat *brk, sl1yo* to the last 2 sts, brk, sl1p wyif. *Do not turn, slide.*

Row 2 MC (RS): K1, repeat *sl1yo, brp* to the last 2 sts, sl1yo, sl1p wyif. Turn work.

Row 3 CC (WS): K1, repeat *brp, sl1yo* to the last 2 sts, brp, sl1p wyif. *Do not turn, slide.*

Row 4 MC (WS): K1, repeat *sl1yo, brk* to the last 2 sts, sl1yo, sl1p wyif. Turn work.

Repeat Rows 1–4 a further 8 (8) 8 (9) 8 (8) 10 (10) 10 times, until you have 19 (19) 19 (21) 19 (19) 23 (23) 23 brioche rows in CC1, counted after the picked up stitches.

LEFT NECK INCREASES

Now increase stitches for the neckline at the *beginning* of every RS row worked in CC.

Row 1 CC (RS): K1, brk, sl1yo, brkyobrk, sl1yo, repeat *brk, sl1yo* until the last 2 sts, brk, sl1p wyif. *Do not turn, slide.*

Row 2 MC (RS): K1, sl1yo, brp, sl1yo, p1, repeat *sl1yo, brp* to the last 2 sts, sl1yo, sl1p wyif. Turn work.

Row 3 CC (WS): K1, repeat *brp, sl1yo* to the last 2 sts, brp, sl1p wyif. *Do not turn, slide.*

Row 4 MC (WS): K1, repeat *sl1yo, brk* to the last 2 sts, sl1yo, sl1p wyif. Turn work.

Repeat Rows 1–4 a further 3 (3) 3 (4) 4 (4) 5 (5) 5 times until you have **23 (27) 31 (33) 37 (41) 43 (47) 51 sts**. Break yarns and place the sts onto a stitch holder.

RIGHT SHOULDER

Remember stitches are picked up according to the brioche ribs on the back, picking up and knitting 1 st in MC followed by 1 st in CC.

With the RS facing you, start picking up sts from the right edge and repeat *using MC pick up and knit 1, using CC1 pick up and knit 1* until you have 14 (18) 22 (22) 26 (30) 30 (34) 38 sts on your needle, using CC1 pick up and knit the last st as well. You now have **15 (19) 23 (23) 27 (31) 31 (35) 39 sts** in total.

Set-up Row CC (WS): K1, repeat *p1, sl1yo* to the last 2 sts, p1, sl1p wyif. *Do not turn, slide.*

Set-up Row MC (WS): K1, repeat *sl1yo, brk* to the last 2 sts, sl1yo, sl1p wyif. Turn work.

Row 1 CC (RS): K1, repeat *brk, sl1yo* to the last 2 sts, brk, sl1p wyif. *Do not turn, slide.*

Row 2 MC (RS): K1, repeat *sl1yo, brp* to the last 2 sts, sl1yo, sl1p wyif. Turn work.

Row 3 CC (WS): K1, repeat *brp, sl1yo* to the last 2 sts, brp, sl1p wyif. *Do not turn, slide.*

Row 4 MC (WS): K1, repeat *sl1yo, brk* to the last 2 sts, sl1yo, sl1p wyif. Turn work.

Repeat Rows 1–4 a further 8 (8) 8 (9) 8 (8) 10 (10) 10 times, until you have 19 (19) 19 (21) 19 (19) 23 (23) 23 brioche rows in CC1, counted after the picked up stitches.

RIGHT NECK INCREASES

Increase stitches for the neckline at *the end* of every RS row worked in CC.

Row 1 CC (RS): K1, repeat repeat *brk, sl1yo* to the last 4 sts, **brkyobrk**, sl1yo, brk, sl1p wyif. *Do not turn, slide.*

Row 2 MC (RS): K1, repeat *sl1yo, brp* to the last 6 sts, sl1yo, **p1**, sl1yo, brp, sl1yo, sl1p wyif. Turn work.

Row 3 CC (WS): K1, repeat *brp, sl1yo* to the last 2 sts, brp, sl1p wyif. **Do not turn, slide.**

Row 4 MC (WS): K1, repeat *sl1yo, brk* to the last 2 sts, sl1yo, sl1p wyif. Turn work.

Repeat Rows 1–4 a further 3 (3) 3 (4) 4 (4) 5 (5) 5 times, until you have **23 (27) 31 (33) 37 (41) 43 (47) 51 sts**.

FRONT SECTION

Now join both shoulders as follows:

Row 1 CC (RS): K1, repeat *brk, sl1yo* to the last 2 sts, brk, p1. Turn work. With CC1 cast on 11 (11) 11 (11) 11 (11) 13 (13) 13 sts using the knitted cast-on method. Turn again and continue with the sts on hold (which are for the left shoulder): K1, repeat *brk, sl1yo* to the last 2 sts, brk, sl1p wyif. *Do not turn, slide.*

Row 2 MC (RS): K1, repeat *sl1yo, brp* 10 (12) 14 (15) 17 (19) 20 (22) 24 times in total, repeat *sl1yo, p1* 7 (7) 7 (7) 7 (7) 8 (8) 8 times in total, repeat *sl1yo, brp* to the last 2 sts, sl1yo, sl1p wyif. Turn work. You now have 57 (65) 73 (77) 85 (93) 99 (107) 115 sts in total.

Row 3 CC (WS): K1, repeat *brp, sl1yo* to the last 2 sts, brp, sl1p wyif. *Do not turn, slide.*

Row 4 MC (WS): K1, repeat *sl1yo, brk* to the last 2 sts, sl1yo, sl1p wyif. Turn work.

Row 5 CC (RS): K1, repeat *brk, sl1yo* to the last 2 sts, brk, sl1p wyif. *Do not turn, slide.*

Row 6 MC (RS): K1, repeat *sl1yo, brp* to the last 2 sts, sl1yo, sl1p wyif. Turn work.

Rows 7 + 8: Repeat **Rows 3 + 4** as above one more time.

Repeat Row 5–8 0 (0) 0 (0) 0 (0) 1 (1) 0 more time(s).

CHART 2

Continue working in brioche stitch and, *at the same time*, working **Chart 2** (see pages 95 + 97 + 99) in your chosen size, starting with Row 1. Remember, charts only show CC rows. Add a MC row after every CC row.

ARMHOLE INCREASES

On **Row 27 (29) 29 (29) 29 (29) 29 (31) 33 of Chart 2**, begin working armhole increases by increasing 2 sts and, on **Row 35 (37) 37 (39) 39 (39) 41 (43) 45 of Chart 2,** increasing 3 sts at the beginning and the end of each RS row and, *at the same time*, change colours as indicated in the chart. The armhole increases are worked the same way as for the back.

BODY

After finishing the armhole increases, there is a slight change in the pattern. Continue knitting **Chart 2** to create the intarsia pattern and, *at the same time*, repeat **Rows 1–4** as described for the back.

After finishing **Chart 2** in your chosen size, cut off MC, leaving a tail of approx. 60–80cm (23½–31½in) for sewing the side seam later. As for the back, to avoid the rib becoming too tight, you now increase 2 sts in every 4th brioche stitch for the bottom rib in CC only.

Changing colours as in the previous row, knit the next row as follows:

Row 1 CC (RS): K1, sl1yo, repeat *(brk, sl1yo) 3 times, brkyobrk, sl1yo* until the last 5 (5) 5 (5) 5 (5) 7 (7) 7 sts, repeat *brk, sl1yo* 2 (2) 2 (2) 2 (2) 3 (3) 3 times, sl1p wyif. Turn work.

Row 2 CC (WS): K2tog (the first st together with the brioche st), p1, repeat *brk, p1* 2 (2) 2 (2) 2 (2) 3 (3) 3 times in total, work *k1, p1, (brk, p1) 4 times* until the end of the row. Remember to change colours as in the previous row. You now have **96 (106) 116 (126) 136 (146) 158 (168) 178 sts** in total.

BOTTOM RIBBING

The bottom rib is worked using the seamless intarsia method to avoid creating a bulky seam on the rib. Transfer all the stitches for the back from the stitch holder onto your needle, placing them after the stitches for the front, so you can knit the front and back rib in one row. Work on a circular needle as you will work the rib using the Magic Loop technique. The intarsia motif will not change, so no colour chart is needed, simply change colours as you did in the last row of Charts 1 + 2.

SET-UP ROW

Change to 3mm (US 2.5) circular needles.

Set-up Row CC (RS): Repeat *k1, p1* across the CC3 front sts, followed by the CC4 front and back sts (which joins the front and back at the right side of the garment) and, to knit the CC3 back sts, join a new CC3 ball. At the end of the row, place a marker, between the front and back stitches, which marks the beginning and end of your row, and turn. Note that you now have two fields of CC3 flanking the marker (one at the start of the front, one at the end of the back), each worked in a separate ball of CC3 yarn.

SEAMLESS INTARSIA SECTION

Seamless intarsia looks as though it is knitted in the round because you are working on a tubular piece of knitting on circular needles. However, you work back and forth across the RS and WS. See page 31 for further information. The following step-by-step instructions and their corresponding pictures provide guidance on how to make the crucial first wraps that join the work in the round. You continue working as established here to complete the ribbing. Note that the pictures show a mocked-up example that is smaller than the vest, to make it easy to see the technique.

Tip: If you have trouble knitting the bottom rib with the seamless intarsia technique, you could also knit the front and back ribs separately and join them together with the side seams. At the armhole ribs, it is easier to get the hang of the seamless intarsia technique, as the front and back are already joined in the round to form the armhole.

Row 1 CC (WS): Wrap yarns for a WS row (as explained in step 1, right), repeat *k1, p1* until the end of the row (to your marker) while, *at the same time*, changing colours to match the motif (following step 2, right), *turn* and pull on the working yarn to complete the intarsia join (following step 3, right).

Working a WS row: Before you begin knitting the row, lay your knitting down in front of you and untangle all the balls.

1. Hold your working yarn upwards to help wrap the yarns. Pick up the CC3 yarn used to knit the colour field flanking the marker on the front (which is at the other end of the colour field from the marker). Wrap it around your working yarn **counterclockwise** (bring it to the right, around the back, over to the left and to front of your working yarn – see pic, wrap A).

2. Continue knitting using your working yarn (see pic). For these first few stitches, pull the working yarn taut (but not too tight). This will help create an invisible join. Don't worry about the long float created by the wrap – this will resolve soon! Whenever you come to a colour change, twist both yarns using a regular intarsia join. When you reach the final join, twist your working yarn with the new yarn, which is connected to the wrap (wrap A) by the long float. To do so, pull the float slightly out of the wrap to lengthen it, which will make twisting and knitting easier. Once you've made this final intarsia join, continue knitting with the float section of CC3 to the end of the row

3. When you reach the end of the row, to eliminate any remaining float, first move all yarns out of the way, then pull the working yarn tight to create a regular intarsia join.

1.

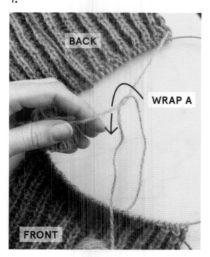

2.

3.

Row 2 CC (RS): Wrap the yarns for a RS row (as explained in step 4, below), repeat *k1, p1* until the end of the row, remembering to change the colours to match the motif (following step 5 below), *turn* and pull on the working yarn to complete the intarsia join (following step 6, below).

Working a RS row: Before you begin knitting the row, lay your knitting down in front of you and untangle all balls.

4. Hold your working yarn upwards to help wrap the yarns. Pick up the CC3 yarn used to knit the colour field flanking the marker on the back (which is at the other end of the colour field from the marker). Wrap it around your working yarn **clockwise** (bring it to the left, around the back, over to the right and to the front of your working yarn – see pic, wrap B) .

5. Continue knitting with your working yarn (see pic). Again, don't be concerned by the long float created by the wrap. Whenever you come to a colour change, twist both yarns using a regular intarsia join. When you reach the final join, twist your working yarn with the new yarn, which is connected to the wrap (wrap B) by the long float. To do so, pull the float slightly out of the wrap to lengthen it, which will make twisting and knitting easier. Once you've made this final intarsia join, continue knitting with the float section of CC3 to the end of the row

6. Move all yarns out of the way and pull your working yarn tight to eliminate the float and create a regular intarsia join.

Repeat Rows 1 + 2 as above four more times.

Row 11 CC (WS): Wrap the yarns as for a WS row, repeat *k1, sl1p wyif* until the end of the row, turn.

Row 12 CC (RS): Wrap the yarns as for a RS row, repeat *k1, sl1p wyif* until the end of the row, turn.

CAST (BIND) OFF

Cast (bind) off using your preferred method. This could, for example, be the Italian Bind-off or a stretchy sewn bind-off variation worked as follows: Cut off all yarns, leaving a tail approx. 1.5 times longer than your colour fields for binding off. Thread your yarn onto a tapestry needle.

Step 1: Working from WS, insert your tapestry needle purlwise into the first three sts on your left hand needle, coming out at the front. Drop the first st off the needle.

Repeat Step 1 until the end of the row.

Note: To align the colour changes, change to the next colour when there are 2 sts remaining of the old colour on your left needle. Drop your old colour at the WS, take your new colour from the WS as well and continue repeating Step 1.

At the end of the row, when there are only 2 sts on your left needle remaining, pick up the first stitch of the beginning of your row and place it on your left needle as well, behind the 2 remaining stitches. To join your cast off in round, repeat Step 1 a further time, pick up the second stitch in the same way and repeat Step 1 a further time.

4.

5.

6.

SIDE SEAMS

Using MC and starting from the bottom up, close up the side seams using mattress stitch. Insert your needle below the CC stitch on the right hand side of the seam and the corresponding MC yarnover on the left hand side of the seam before the edge stitch, as shown in the pictures here, so that the seam creates a MC ridge and is almost invisible from the front.

ARMHOLE RIBBING

The armhole ribbing is knitted the same way as the bottom rib by using the seamless intarsia method to continue the motif of the body. When picking up and knitting stitches for the armhole, change the CC yarns according to the motif of your vest.

Using 3mm (US 2.5) circular needles and CC1, pick up and knit stitches as follows. Beginning at the centre of the underarm, pick up and knit 1 stitch in every edge stitch and picking up a few extra stitches at the bottom of the armhole and the shoulder join, ie. the back-to-front corner, to round the corners. When picking up and knitting stitches, insert your needle below both legs of the edge stitches. You now have **124 (128) 130 (134) 134 (134) 146 (150) 154 sts** in total.

Place a marker in the middle underneath the armhole to mark the beginning and end of your row and turn.
Row 1 CC (WS): Wrap the yarns as for a WS row, repeat *k1, p1* to the end of the row, remembering to change the colours to match the motif. Turn work.
Row 2 CC (RS): Wrap the yarns as for a RS row, repeat *k1, p1* to the end of the row. Turn work.
Repeat Rows 1 + 2 three more times.
Row 9 CC (WS): Wrap the yarns as for a WS row, repeat *k1, sl1p wyif* to the end of the row. Turn work.
Row 10 CC (RS): Wrap the yarns as for a RS row, repeat *k1, sl1p wyif* to the end of the row. Turn work.
Cast (bind) off the same way as for the body ribbing, on a WS row.

NECK RIBBING

Next, add a folded rib at the neck, using only CC1. Using 3mm (US 2.5) circular needles and CC1, pick up and knit stitches as follows. Beginning at the left shoulder seam, pick up and knit 1 stitch in every edge stitch and the cast-on stitches and pick up and knit quite a few extra stitches at the shoulder joins and the cast-on corners to round the corners. When picking up stitches, insert your needle below both legs of the edge stitch. You now have **102 (102) 104 (112) 112 (114) 128 (130) 132 sts** in total.

Round 1: Repeat *k1, p1* across all sts.

Rounds 2–9: Repeat Round 1.

Round 10: Repeat *k1, sl1p wyif* across all sts.

Rounds 11 + 12: Repeat Round 10.

Rounds 13–20: Repeat Round 1.

On the following round, cast (bind) off the stitches and, *at the same time*, secure the rib to the inside of the neckline by knitting every other stitch together with a stitch picked up from the beginning of the neck rib.

Tip: Turning your vest inside out and working from the WS makes this process easier.

Round 21: Repeat *pick up 1 st from the first row of the neck rib and place it onto your left needle, knit the st together with the next st on your left needle and cast off 1 st, p1 and cast off a further st* until the end of the round.

FINISHING

Weave in all ends, gently wash your Along The Coast Vest and block it according to the measurements of your chosen size.

CHART 1 BACK

Note: Charts only show CC rows. Add an MC row after every CC row. Armhole increases are not marked in the chart, but described in the written instructions.

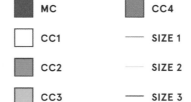

MC

CC1

CC2

CC3

CC4

— SIZE 1

— SIZE 2

— SIZE 3

Note: See page 13 for notes on reading these charts before you begin following them.

EDGE STITCH: See special techniques.

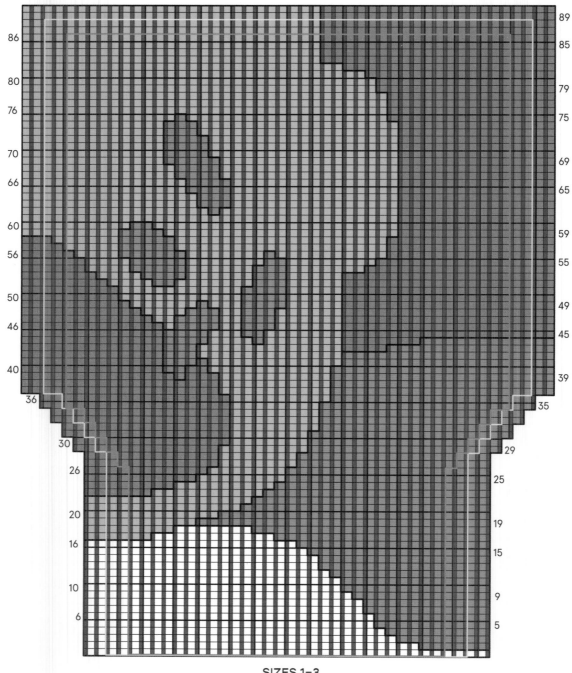

SIZES 1–3

Along the Coast Vest

CHART 2 FRONT

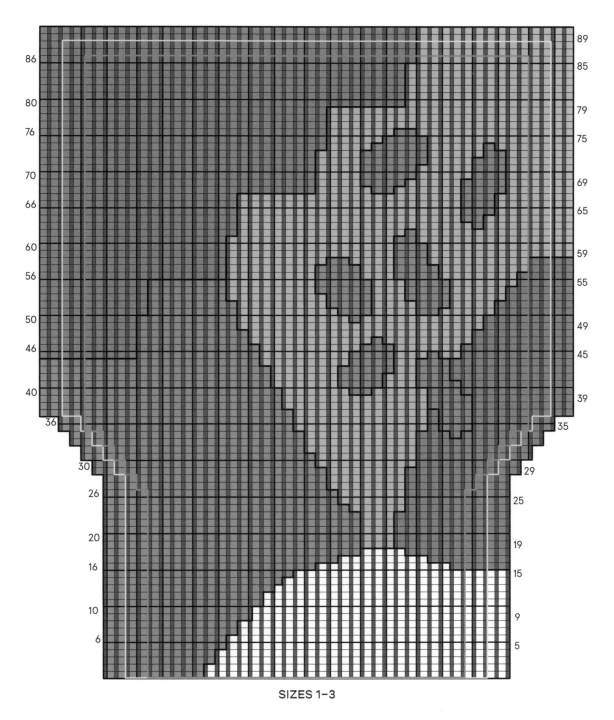

SIZES 1–3

CHART 1 BACK

See page 94 for key.

——— **SIZE 4**   ——— **SIZE 6**

——— **SIZE 5**

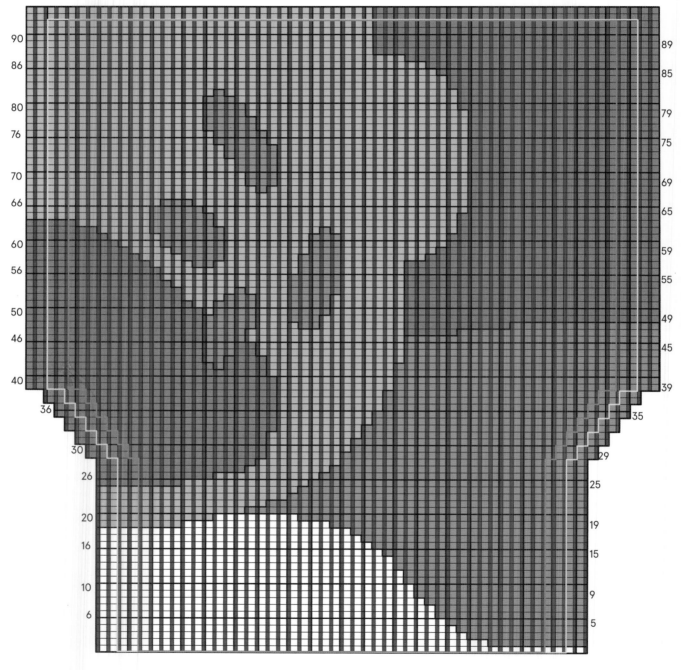

SIZES 4–6

Along the Coast Vest

CHART 2 FRONT

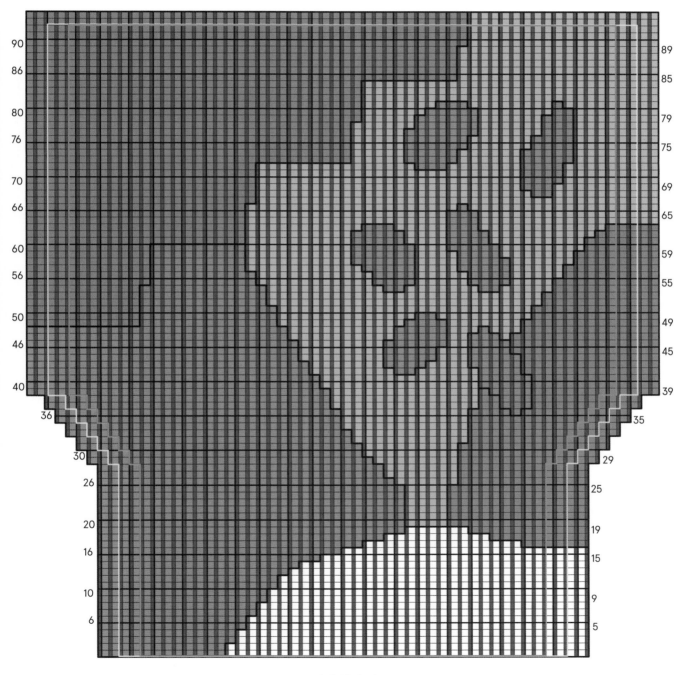

SIZES 4-6

CHART 1 BACK

See page 94 for key.

—— SIZE 7

—— SIZE 8

—— SIZE 9

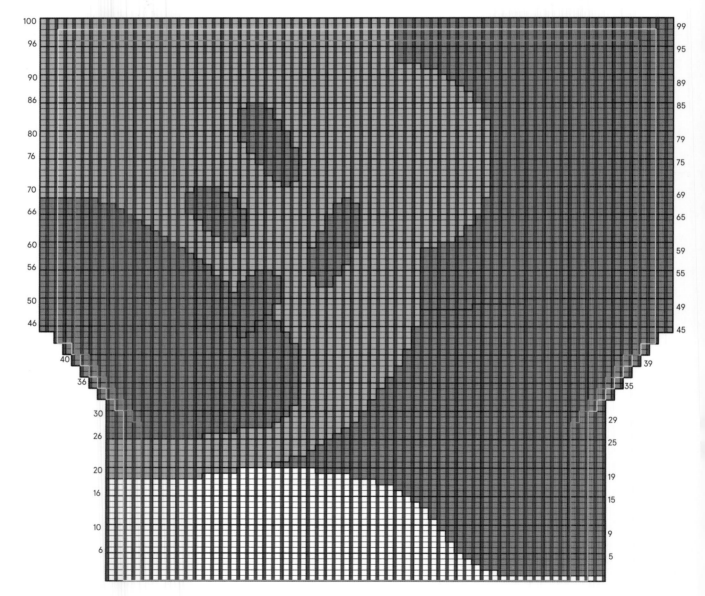

SIZES 7–9

CHART 2 FRONT

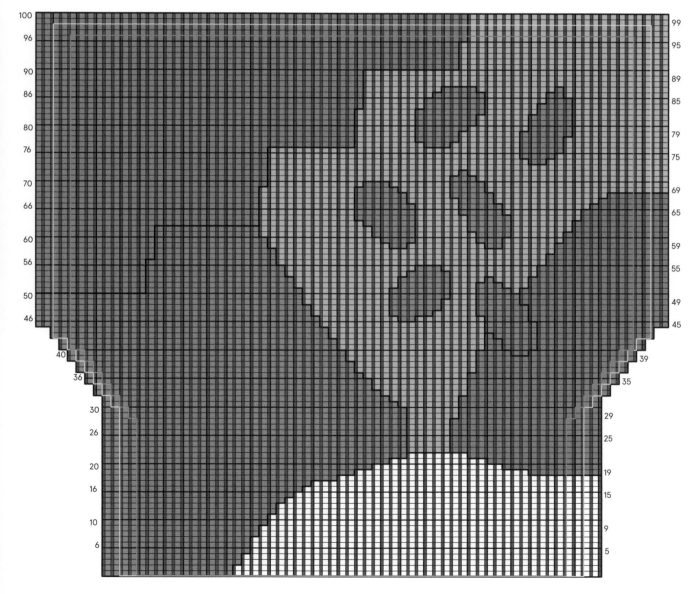

SIZES 7–9

Between Ebb and Flow Top

The Between Ebb And Flow Top is inspired by coastal tides, which I find fascinating because they are constantly in motion, yet steadily so. I can't say what impresses me more. The calm, smooth-as-a-mirror surface of the water at low tide, reflecting the clouds, and the exposed textures of the sandbanks, and how far out you must walk before the sea surrounds you. Or, the moments when the flood comes, when the sea returns at high tide, and the waves rage and almost sweep you away. The intarsia motif of the Between Ebb And Flow Top plays with these contrasts, with two shades of a colour, one lighter and one darker, the separation that is in motion and yet fits together perfectly, and the constant, recurring movement of ebb and flow.

#betweenebbandflowtop

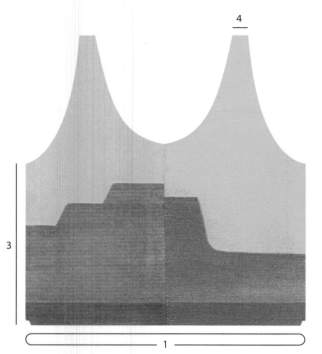

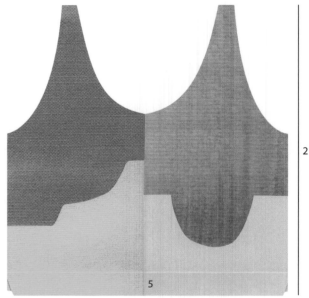

CONSTRUCTION

The Between Ebb And Flow Top is a sleeveless top with a simple silhouette and a colour-block design made from four shades. It is knitted from the top down in stocking (stockinette) stitch, using the intarsia technique to create a simple abstract motif at the front and back.

First, knit each strap separately, increasing on both sides. After joining the straps, knit the front and back with the intarsia motif, still continuing the colour-block design. After adding a 2 x 2 rib at the bottom, sew together the side seams, except for at the ribs, to create a split hem at the bottom.

SKILL LEVEL

●●○○○

SIZES

Sizes 1 (2) 3 (4) 5 (6) 7 (8) 9 are designed to fit a bust circumference of: 76 (86) 96 (106) 116 (126) 136 (146) 156cm / 30 (34) 38 (42) 46 (50) 54 (57) 61in

The Between Ebb And Flow Top is designed to be worn with approx. 3–16cm (1¼–6¼in) positive ease. Measure your bust circumference to choose a suitable size.

Tip: If you'd prefer to wear your top as a layering piece, I'd recommend sizing up one size.

FINISHED MEASUREMENTS

1. **Bust circumference:** 86 (95) 107 (116) 124 (137) 145 (154) 166cm / 33¾ (37½) 42 (45½) 48¾ (54) 57 (60¾) 65¼in
2. **Total length:** 50 (50.5) 51.5 (52) 52.5 (53.5) 53.5 (54) 54.5cm / 19¾ (20) 20¼ (20½) 20¾ (21) 21 (21¼) 21½in
3. **Length, bottom hem to armhole:** 28cm (11in)
4. **Strap width:** Approx. 5.3 (5.3) 5.8 (6.3) 6.3 (6.8) 6.8 (7.3) 7.3cm / 2 (2) 2¼ (2½) 2½ (2¾) 2¾ (3) 3in

Note: The sides of the straps roll in when worn, making them a bit narrower in use.

5. **Bottom rib:** Approx. 5cm / 2in

YARN

Two strands of lace-weight yarn held double or, alternatively, use one strand of a 4-ply (fingering weight) yarn. You will need four shades. You will also need waste yarn for casting on.

Please note, that these quantities are only estimates. These quantities are for if you are using the yarn held double. If using a single strand, halve the quantities.

SAMPLE 1

C1   C2   C3   C4

SAMPLE 2

C1   C2   C3   C4

C1: 213 (238) 264 (289) 323 (357) 391 (425) 451m
/ 232 (260) 289 (316) 353 (391) 428 (465) 493yds
C2: 170 (204) 238 (247) 281 (315) 332 (374) 408m
/ 186 (223) 260 (270) 307 (344) 363 (409) 446yds
C3: 255 (281) 306 (349) 374 (408) 442 (476) 510m
/ 279 (307) 335 (381) 409 (446) 484 (521) 558yds
C4: 196 (230) 264 (281) 315 (357) 374 (408) 451m
/ 214 (251) 289 (307) 344 (391) 409 (446) 493yds

Yarn used in sample: ITO Kinu (100 per cent silk noil,
425m / 464yds) – 50g / 1¾oz), held double.

Colourway for sample 1 (shown on page 101):
C1: 359 Persimmon, 1 (1) 1 (1) 1 (1) 2 (2) 2 cone(s)
C2: 393 Pale Blue, 1 (1) 1 (1) 1 (1) 1 (1) 2 cone(s)
C3: 491 Mint, 1 (1) 1 (1) 1 (1) 2 (2) 2 cone(s)
C4: 487 Mustard, 1 (1) 1 (1) 1 (1) 1 (2) 2 cone(s)

Colourway for sample 2 (shown on page 104):
C1: 394 Aqua
C2: 399 Peach
C3: 360 Cayenne Red
C4: 374 Pool Green

NEEDLES

3mm (US 2.5) circular needles, or size needed to obtain
the correct tension (gauge), for the body and 2.5mm
(US 1.5) circular needles for the ribbing.

TENSION (GAUGE)

19 sts x 31 rows to 10 x 10cm (4 x 4in) in stocking
(stockinette) stitch, measured after washing and
blocking.

SPECIAL TECHNIQUES

INTARSIA JOIN
See pages 26–27.

I-CORD EDGE STITCH
First 3 sts of every row: K1, sl1p wyif, k1.
Last 3 sts of every row: Sl1p wyif, k1, sl1p wyif.

PATTERN

BACK
The back and the front are worked in the same way, but
with different motifs on both sides. Follow **Chart 1** for
the back and **Chart 2** for the front. Later, you can
decide which motif you want to wear to the front, as
the construction is identical.
First, work both straps separately, increasing at both
sides. Then join the straps together to work the back with
the intarsia motif.
Optional: You can also knit both straps at the same time,
but apart, by knitting on one circular needle. Follow the
strap 1 instructions using C1 and follow the strap 2
instructions using C2.

STRAP 1
Using 3mm (US 2.5) needles and waste yarn, cast on
10 (10) 11 (12) 12 (13) 13 (14) 14 sts using a provisional cast
on method. Change to C1, but leave a tail of approx.
30cm (12in) for grafting the straps later.
Row 1 (RS): K to the end of the row.
Row 2 (WS): P to the end of the row.
Repeat Rows 1 + 2 a further 10 (7) 6 (5) 3 (2) 2 (1) 0 times.

NECK AND ARMHOLE INCREASES
Begin working neck increases by increasing 1 st at the
beginning of a RS row and armhole increases by
increasing 1 stitch at the end of a RS row. As the shape of
the neckline and the armholes are slightly different, the
increases are not symmetrical, but worked as follows:

Row 1 (RS): K3, M1L, k to the last 3 sts, M1R, k3. (2 sts
increased)
Row 2 (WS): P to the end of the row.
Row 3 (RS): K3, M1L, k to the end of the row. (1 st
increased)

Row 4 (WS): Repeat Row 2 once more.
Row 5 (RS): Repeat Row 3 once more. (1 st increased)
Row 6 (WS): Repeat Row 2 once more.
Repeat Rows 1–6 a further 2 (3) 2 (3) 3 (3) 2 (2) 1 times. You now have **22 (26) 23 (28) 28 (29) 25 (26) 22 sts** in total.
Now continue as follows:
Row 1 (RS): K3, M1L, k to the last 3 sts, M1R, k3. (2 sts increased)
Row 2 (WS): P to the end of the row.
Row 3 (RS): K3, M1L, k to the end of the row. (1 st increased)
Row 4 (WS): Repeat Row 2 once more.
Repeat Rows 1–4 a further 2 (3) 4 (2) 4 (3) 2 (2) 2 times. You now have **31 (38) 38 (37) 43 (41) 34 (35) 31 sts** in total.
Repeat Rows 1 + 2 only a further 2 (0) 3 (5) 4 (8) 14 (15) 20 times. You now have **35 (38) 44 (47) 51 (57) 62 (65) 71 sts** in total.
Don't cut C1, but place all stitches on a stitch holder to knit strap 2 before joining both straps.

STRAP 2
Strap 2 is knitted in the same way as strap 1, but with increases mirrored.
Using 3mm (US 2.5) needles and waste yarn, cast on **10 (10) 11 (12) 12 (13) 13 (14) 14 sts** using a provisional cast-on method. Change to C2, but leave a tail of approx. 30cm (12in) for grafting the straps later.
Row 1 (RS): K to the end of the row.
Row 2 (WS): P to the end of the row.
Repeat Rows 1 + 2 a further 10 (7) 6 (5) 3 (2) 2 (1) 0 times.

NECK AND ARMHOLE INCREASES
Again, work neck and armhole increases by increasing 1 st at the beginning and/or the end of a RS row as specified below.
Row 1 (RS): K3, M1L, k to the last 3 sts, M1R, k3. (2 sts increased)
Row 2 (WS): P to the end of the row.
Row 3 (RS): K to the last 3 sts, M1R, k3. (1 st increased)
Row 4 (WS): Repeat Row 2 once moire.
Row 5 (RS): Repeat Row 3 once more. (1 st increased)
Row 6 (WS): Repeat Row 2 once more.
Repeat Rows 1–6 a further 2 (3) 2 (3) 3 (3) 2 (2) 1 times. You now have **22 (26) 23 (28) 28 (29) 25 (26) 22 sts** in total.
Now continue as follows:
Row 1 (RS): K3, M1L, k to the last 3 sts, M1R, k3. (2 sts increased)

Row 2 (WS): P to the end of the row.

Row 3 (RS): K to the last 3 sts, M1R, k3. (1 st increased)

Row 4 (WS): Repeat Row 2 once more.

Repeat Rows 1–4 a further 2 (3) 4 (2) 4 (3) 2 (2) 2 times. You now have **31 (38) 38 (37) 43 (41) 34 (35) 31 sts** in total.

Repeat Rows 1 + 2 a further 2 (0) 3 (5) 4 (8) 14 (15) 20 times. You now have **35 (38) 44 (47) 51 (57) 62 (65) 71 sts** in total.

BACK SECTION

Now join both straps. Transfer the stitches of Strap 1 from the stitch holder back onto your left needle, behind the stitches for Strap 2.

Row 1 (RS): Work the stitches of Strap 2 first: K3, M1L, k to the last 3 sts remaining of Strap 2, M1R, k3. Now, twist C2 and C1, where both straps meet, to create a regular intarsia join, and continue working the stitches of Strap 1 as follows: K3, M1L, k to the last 3 sts, M1R, k3. (4 sts increased) You now have **74 (80) 92 (98) 106 (118) 128 (134) 146 sts** in total.

Row 2 (WS): P to the end of the row, changing colours as in the previous row (ie. at the centre), using the intarsia technique.

ARMHOLE INCREASES

Continue working armhole increases by increasing 1 st at the beginning and the end of every RS row, *at the same time* changing colours as in the previous row (ie. at the centre).

Row 1 (RS): K3, M1L, k to the last 3 st, M1R, k3. (2 sts increased)

Row 2 (WS): P to the end of the row.

Repeat Rows 1 + 2 a further 4 (5) 5 (6) 6 (6) 5 (6) 6 times. You now have **84 (92) 104 (112) 120 (132) 140 (148) 160 sts** in total.

Note: Place removable markers on both sides after finishing the armhole increases to mark the beginning of your side seams.

CHART 1

Continue knitting in stocking (stockinette) stitch with the intarsia join down the centre for 8 rows.

Now begin working **Chart 1** (see pages 106 + 108 + 110) in stocking stitch.

After finishing Chart 1, continue in stocking stitch for 14 rows until your work measures approx. 23cm (9in) from the armhole or until the desired length. (Note that any extra length added is not accounted for in the amount of yarn required.)

BOTTOM RIBBING

Now, add a split hem at the bottom in 2 x 2 rib. To add a nice selvedge to the split hem, work an I-cord edge stitch on both sides of the rib, using the first and last 3 sts of your row. Using 2.5mm (US 1.5) needles, knit the rib as follows, remembering to change colours as in the previous row.

Row 1 (RS): K1, sl1p wyif, k1, repeat *p2, k2* to the last 5 sts, p2, sl1p wyif, k1, sl1p wyif.

Row 2 (WS): K1, sl1p wyif, k1, repeat *k2, p2* to the last 5 sts, k2, sl1p wyif, k1, sl1p wyif.

Repeat Rows 1 + 2 a further 9 times until the ribbing measures approx. 5cm (2in).

Cast (bind) off using your preferred method.

Optional: To avoid the cast-off edge becoming too tight, use your main needle size for the cast off.

FRONT

Repeat the instructions for the back, but instead of following Chart 1 as described, follow **Chart 2** (see pages 107 + 109 + 111) instead and use **C3** for strap 1 and **C4** for strap 2.

SEWING THE SIDE SEAMS

Sew together the side seams, using the mattress stitch. Leave out the rib stitches to create a split hem.

JOINING THE STRAPS

Pin both straps together and try the top on to make sure that you like the length. You can unravel a few plain rows or work a few rows in stocking (stockinette) stitch to make the straps shorter or longer. If you are happy with the length, sew together the strap stitches by grafting them together in stocking (stockinette) stitch.

FINISHING

Sew in all ends. For example, use the duplicate stitch method to sew in ends on the WS. If you are working with a delicate yarn held double, I'd recommend weaving in both yarn ends separately to avoid creating too much extra bulk.

Gently wash your Between Ebb And Flow Top and block it according to the measurements of your chosen size.

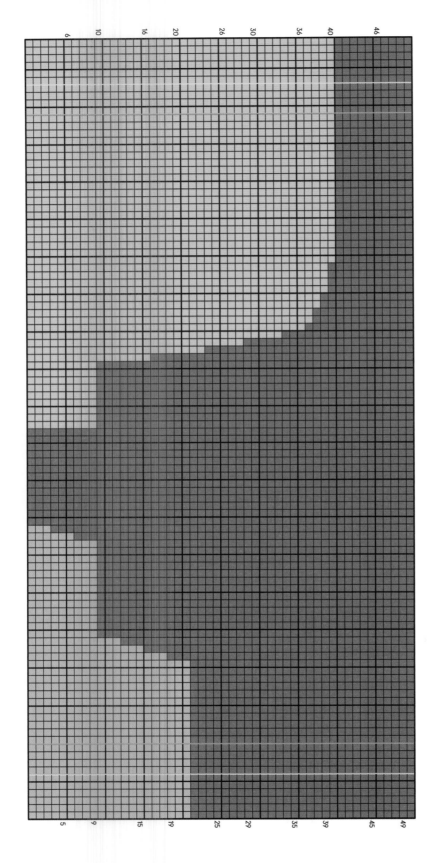

CHART 1 BACK

SIZES 1–3

Note: See page 13 for notes on reading these charts before you begin following them.

⬜ C1	—— SIZE 1
⬜ C2	—— SIZE 2
⬛ C3	—— SIZE 3
⬛ C4	

CHART 2 FRONT

SIZES 1-3

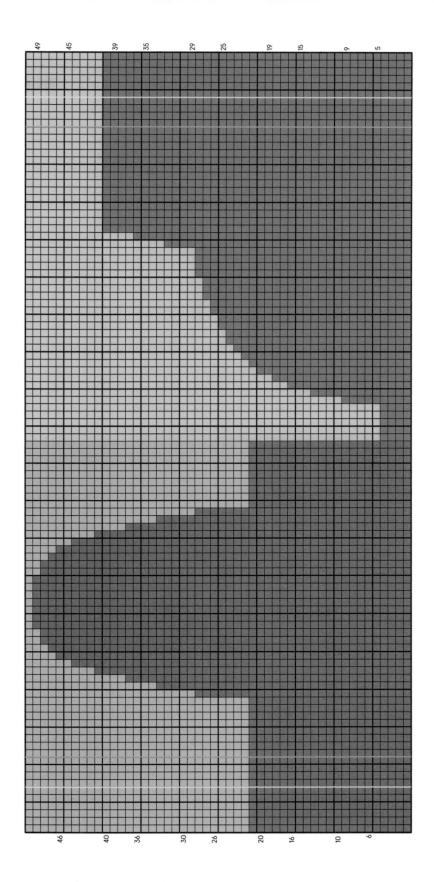

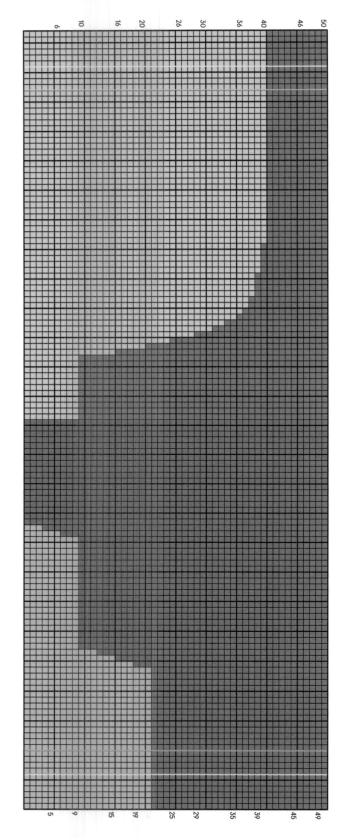

CHART 1 BACK

SIZES 4–6

See page 106 for key.

—— **SIZE 4**

—— **SIZE 5**

—— **SIZE 6**

Between Ebb and Flow Top

CHART 2 FRONT

SIZES 4–6

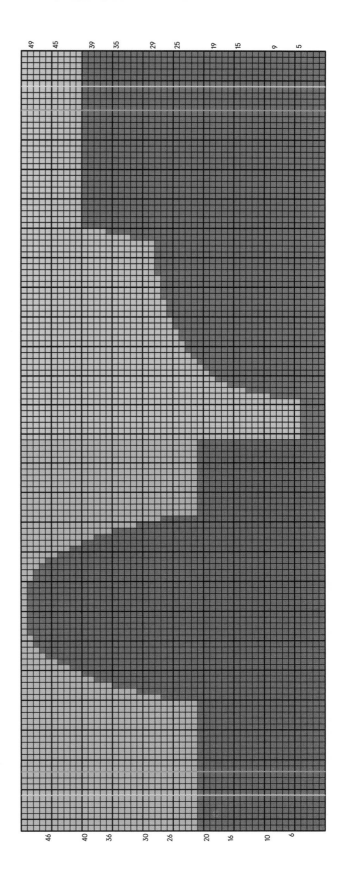

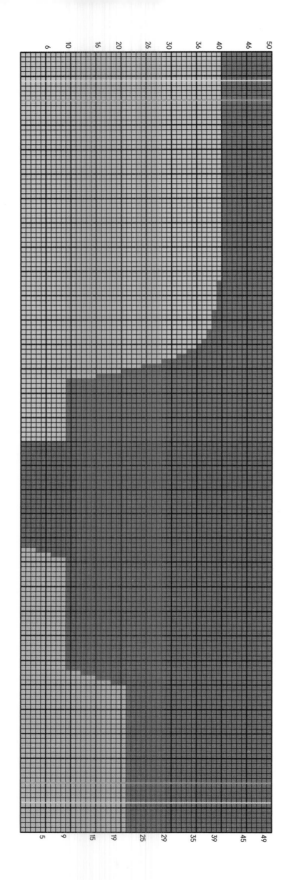

CHART 1 BACK

SIZES 7–9

See page 106 for key.

——— **SIZE 7**

——— **SIZE 8**

——— **SIZE 9**

CHART 2 FRONT

SIZES 7–9

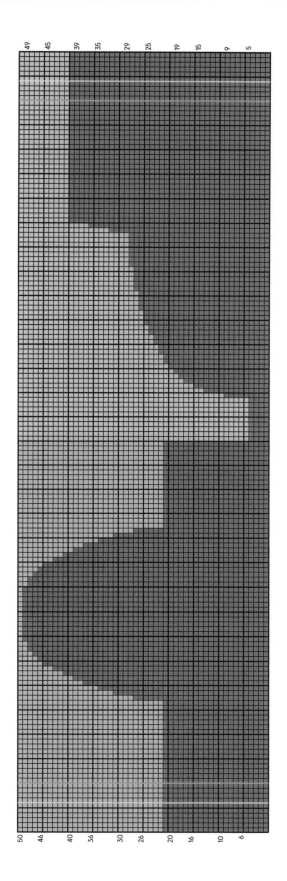

Towards the Sea Tote

The abstract landscape pattern on the Towards the Sea Tote is inspired by the trail to a very special beach. You follow a path that is flanked by rose hip bushes, with purple heather shimmering beyond them. As you reach further up the dunes, sand and beach grasses blend with the heather to form striking textural combinations. When I see the sun peeking over the tops of the dunes, I know I'm almost at the sea and will soon enjoy the expansive view over the horizon.

#towardstheseatote

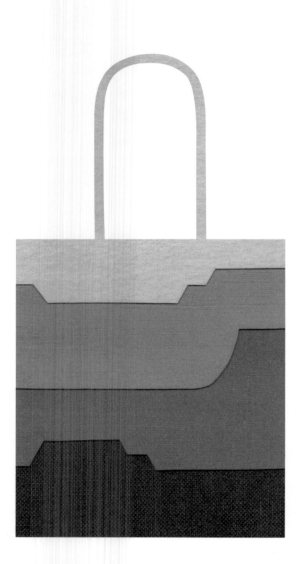

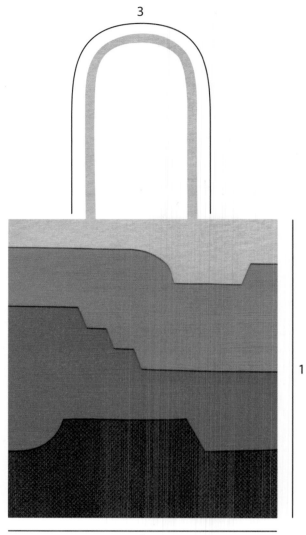

CONSTRUCTION

The Towards The Sea Tote is worked flat in a bobble stitch pattern, using the intarsia technique to create an abstract landscape motif.

The bag is worked from the top down, starting with a double-folded edge for a neat finish. The front and back are knitted separately and grafted together at the base. After closing the side seams, stitches are picked up out of the double folded edge to create double knitted straps, which are then sewn together at the top.

SKILL LEVEL

●●●○○

FINISHED MEASUREMENTS

1. **Height:** 36cm (14¼in)
2. **Width:** 30cm (11¾in)
3. **Length of the straps, measured from the top of the bag:** 57cm (22½in)

YARN

Use a chunky (bulky) weight yarn, for example a blow yarn.

C1: 99m (108yds)
C2: 81m (89yds)
C3: 77m (84yds)
C4: 86m (94yds)

Yarn used in the sample: CaMaRose Snefnug (55 per cent baby alpaca, 35 per cent organic cotton and 10 per cent extra fine merino wool, 110m / 120yds – 50g / 1¾oz).
C1: 7966 Lys Pudder, 1 skein
C2: 7386 Pudder, 1 skein
C3: 7864 Havgrøn, 1 skein
C4: 7885 Mørkegrøn, 1 skein

NEEDLES

4.5mm (US 7) circular needles, or size necessary to obtain the correct tension (gauge), for the bag and 3.5mm (US 4) circular needles and DPNs for the folded edge and straps.

TENSION (GAUGE)

17 sts x 24 rows to 10 x 10cm (4 x 4in) in bobble stitch pattern (see below), measured after washing and blocking.

SPECIAL TECHNIQUES

INTARSIA JOIN
See pages 26–27.

CARRYING YARNS AND BINDING FLOATS
See pages 28–29.

BOBBLE STITCH
1. Work as follows in the same st: K1, repeat *yo, k1* 3 times, so you have 7 loops from the one stitch.
2. Using your left needle tip, pass the second stitch on your right needle over the first stitch, which is closest to the needle tip. Repeat until 1 st remains.
3. With yarn in front, lift the loop from the stitch below your bobble stitch from the WS onto your right needle as well.
4. With yarn in back, insert your left hand needle into both stitches and knit them together through the back loop.

3.

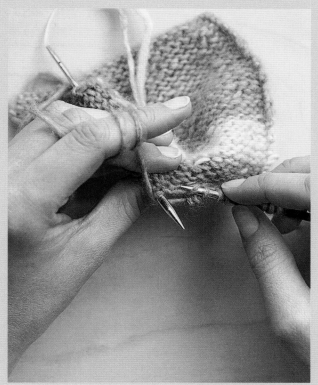

4.

BOBBLE STITCH PATTERN

Cast on a multiple of 5 sts plus 2 sts, using the long-tail cast-on method.

Set-up Row (WS): P to the end of the row.

Row 1 (RS): K to the end of the row.

Row 2 (WS): P to the end of the row.

Row 3 (RS): K3, repeat *work a bobble stitch, k4* to the last 4 sts, work a bobble stitch, k3.

Row 4 (WS): P to the end of the row.

Row 5 (RS): K to the end of the row.

Row 6 (WS): P to the end of the row.

Repeat Rows 1–6 until your swatch is big enough to check your tension.

PATTERN

FRONT

Using 3.5mm (US 4) needles and waste yarn, cast on **52 sts** using a provisional cast-on method.

Row 1 (WS): Using C1, p to the end of the row.

Row 2 (RS): K to the end of the row.

Row 3 (WS): P to the end of the row.

Row 4 (RS): K to the end of the row.

Row 5 (WS): P15. Drop your working yarn and, using waste yarn, p3, continue with your working yarn, thereby creating a small float on the WS, and p16. Drop your working yarn and, using a new strand of waste yarn, p3, continue with your working yarn and p15.

Row 6 (RS): K to the end of the row and knit across the waste yarn sts using your working yarn.

Row 7 (WS): P to the end of the row.

Repeat Rows 6–7 once more.

Place the sts of your provisional cast on onto your right needle. Take both needles in your left hand and place them with the WS of the fabric facing towards each other so that the edge folds in half. The last worked row is at the front towards you and the stitches from the cast on are at the back.

Take 4.5mm (US 7) needles as your new right needle and knit the stitches from both needles together as follows:

Row 1 (RS): Repeat *k tog 1 st from the front needle and 1 st from the back needle* to the end of the row.

Row 2 (WS): P to the end of the row.

Begin working **Chart 1** (see page 118) to create the intarsia pattern and, at the same time, **repeat Rows 1–6** as follows:
Row 1 (RS): K to the end of the row.
Row 2 (WS): P to the end of the row.
Row 3 (RS): K3, repeat *work a bobble stitch, k4* to the last 4 sts, work a bobble stitch, k3.
Row 4 (WS): P to the end of the row.
Row 5 (RS): K to the end of the row.
Row 6 (WS): P to the end of the row.
After finishing Chart 1, break C4 and place the sts on a stitch holder.

BACK
The back is knitted the same way as the front. Repeat the instructions for the front, but, instead of following Chart 1 as described, follow **Chart 2** (see page 119).

CAST (BIND) OFF
Transfer the stitches for the front from the stitch holder back onto your right needle and place both needles with the WS of the fabric facing towards each other. Break C4, leaving a tail of approx 70cm (27½in). Thread the tail onto your tapestry needle and cast off all stitches by grafting the stitches from the front and back together in stocking (stockinette) stitch.

FRONT STRAPS
The straps are knitted by picking up stitches out of the folded edge at your waste yarn stitches. Both front straps will be knitted half way up and grafted together at the top. The straps will be worked in double knitting, therefore pick up the stitches as follows.

STRAP 1
Remove the waste yarn and pick up the loose stitches on two separate double-pointed needles. Towards the back on the WS, pick up 3 loose purl stitches and, towards the front on the RS, pick up 4 knit stitches (2 loose stitches as well as 2 half-loose knit stitches flanking them). Then, using 3.5mm (US 4) needles, with the front of the bag facing you, repeat *slide 1 knit stitch on your right hand needle, slide 1 purl stitch on your right hand needle* 3 times in total. Lastly, slide the 4th knit st on your needle as well. You now have 7 sts in total.

Using 3.5mm (US 4) needles and C1, knit the strap as follows:
Row 1 (RS): Repeat *k1, s1p wyif* to the last st, k1.
Row 2 (WS): Repeat *s1p wyif, k1* to the last st, s1p wyif.
Repeat Rows 1 + 2 a further 49 times or until the strap has your preferred length.
Place all stitches on a stitch holder until you have worked the second strap.

STRAP 2
Repeat the instructions above for the second front strap. Using C1, **repeat Rows 1 + 2** as above 48 times instead, or one less repeat than Strap 1. Cut C1, leaving a tail of approx. 30cm (12in) for grafting the straps together.

First, divide the stitches of the double knit straps so that you can graft both strap halves together in stocking (stockinette) stitch. With the front of the bag facing you, divide them as follows: place all knit stitches on one double-pointed needle and all purl stitches on another. Repeat the process with the stitches of the opposite strap. Now, place both stocking stitch needles with the WS of the fabric facing towards each other, and use the C1 tail to graft the stitches together all the way around with all strap stitches.

BACK STRAPS
Repeat the instructions for the front straps to work the back straps.

FINISHING
First of all, sew in all ends that are not needed for sewing the side seam, for example, by using the duplicate stitch method on the wrong side.

Gently wash your Towards The Sea Tote bag and block it flat according to the given measurements. Blocking the bag before closing the side seams allows your bobbles to remain nice and neat.

SIDE SEAM
Sew together both side seams by stitching together the front and back edges using mattress stitch.

CHART 1 FRONT

Note: See page 13 for notes on reading these charts before you begin following them.

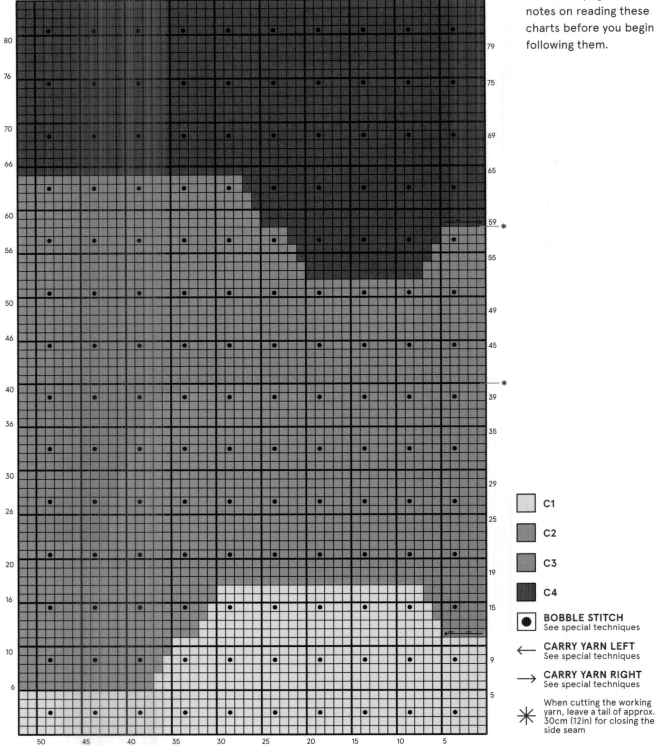

C1

C2

C3

C4

BOBBLE STITCH
See special techniques

CARRY YARN LEFT
See special techniques

CARRY YARN RIGHT
See special techniques

When cutting the working yarn, leave a tail of approx. 30cm (12in) for closing the side seam

CHART 2 BACK

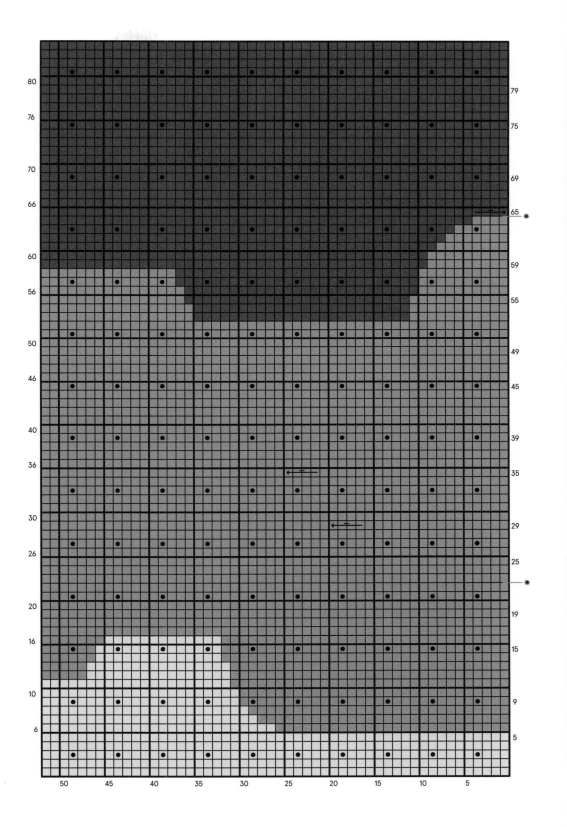

Below the
Horizon Mittens

I enjoy watching the hustle and bustle of the harbour in my hometown, especially during twilight, when the sun is far enough below the horizon for the magical blue hour to begin. If you take a ferry you can enjoy the twinkling of the city's colourful lights from the river. Another favourite vantage point is the top of the highest building in the harbour, from where you get a stunning view of the city's houses and the cranes in the harbour. This vista, in the peaceful atmosphere of the time just before night falls, provided the inspiration for the Below The Horizon Mittens.

#belowthehorizonmittens

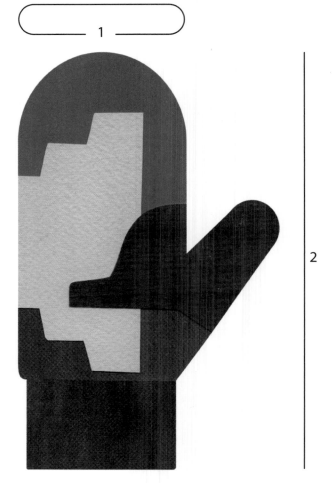

2

CONSTRUCTION

The Below The Horizon Mittens are knitted flat in garter stitch and sewn together at the end. A colourful graphic motif is created using the intarsia technique. Each mitten is knitted from the bottom up, beginning with a 2 x 2 rib, then working the base of the palm, where you increase stitches for the thumb. Next, the thumb is knitted flat, then sewn together, after which you return to the body of the mitten to begin decreasing for the top.

You will knit two mittens with identical construction and almost-identical intarsia patterns, following the charts. When wearing the mittens, the pattern that shows on the palm side of one mitten sits on the back of the hand on the other mitten, and vice versa.

SKILL LEVEL

● ● ○ ○ ○

SIZES

Sizes 1 (2) 3 are designed to fit a hand circumference of: 18 (20) 22cm (7 (7¾) 8¾in).

To choose a suitable size, measure the circumference of the widest part of your hand (which is usually just below the knuckles) and exclude your thumb. Ensure that the measuring tape is neither too loose nor too tight so that the finished mittens fit nicely.

FINISHED MEASUREMENTS

1. **Circumference:** 18.5 (20.5) 22.5cm / 7¼ (8) 9in
2. **Length:** 24.5 (25.5) 26.5cm / 9¾ (10) 10½in

YARN

Chunky (bulky) weight yarn in five shades.
C1: 45 (50) 56m / 49 (55) 61yds
C2: 32 (36) 41m / 35 (39) 45yds
C3: 27 (32) 38m / 30 (35) 41yds
C4: 27 (32) 38m / 30 (35) 41yds
C5: 31 (38) 45m / 34 (41) 49yds

Yarn used in the sample: Biches & Bûches, Le Coton & Alpaca (66 per cent GOTS Cotton and 34 per cent Super Fine Alpaca, 90m / 98yds – 50g / 1¾oz).
C1: Soft Dark Grey, (1 skein)
C2: Light Grey Blue, (1 skein)
C3: Dark Green Grey, (1 skein)
C4: Rose Grey, (1 skein)
C5: Soft Gold, (1 skein)

NEEDLES

4.5mm (US 7) circular needles, or size needed to obtain the correct tension (gauge), for the mittens and 3.5mm (US 4) circular needles for the cuff.

TENSION (GAUGE)

18 sts x 34 rows (17 garter ridges) to 10 x 10cm 4 x 4in) in garter stitch using 4.5mm (US 7), measured after washing and blocking.

READING THE CHARTS

The charts show RS rows only. The intarsia pattern for each odd-numbered row is exactly the same for the following even-numbered row. So, for rows 1 and 2, read the chart row labelled 1 + 2 from right to left for row 1 (RS), then from left to right for row 2 (WS), and so on.

SPECIAL TECHNIQUES

INTARSIA JOIN
See pages 26–27.

CARRYING YARNS AND BINDING FLOATS
See pages 28–29.

GARTER EDGE STITCH
First st of every row: Sl1k.
Last st of every row: K1.

PATTERN

CUFF

First, knit a cuff in 2x2 rib. To avoid the cast-on edge becoming too tight, cast on using the larger needles, then switch to the smaller-sized needles after the cast-on row to knit the cuff.
Using 4.5mm (US 7) needles and C1, cast on **33 (37) 41 sts** using the long-tail cast-on method.
Change to 3.5mm (US 4) needles.
Set-up Row (WS): K2, repeat *p2, k2* until the last 3 sts, p2, k1.
Row 1 (RS): Sl1k, repeat *k2, p2* until the last 4 sts, k2, p1, k1.
Row 2 (WS): Sl1k, k1, repeat *p2, k2* until the last 3 sts, p2, k1.
Repeat Rows 1 + 2 a further 7 (7) 7 times, or until the cuff reaches your preferred length.

MITTEN BASE

Change to 4.5mm (US 7) to knit the mitten in garter stitch. Begin working **Chart 1** (see pages 127–129) in your chosen size to create the intarsia pattern and work the thumb increases, and, *at the same time*, work in garter stitch by repeating **Rows 1 + 2** as follows:
Row 1 (RS): Sl1k, k to the end of the row.
Row 2 (WS): Sl1k, k to the end of the row.
When working the first row of **Chart 1**, place two markers as shown on the chart to indicate the points between which the sts for the thumb will be increased.
Note: See left for notes on reading the charts before you begin following Chart 1.
Thumb increases: Note that increases are made on RS rows only. Therefore, symbols on the chart indicating increases refer to the RS rows (odd-numbered rows) only. You will see on the chart that, on every other RS row, you increase sts for the thumb after the first and before the second marker. Work increase rows as follows while changing colours as indicated on the chart:
Increase rows (RS): Sl1k, knit to the first marker, sm, kfb, k to last st before the second marker, kfb, sm, knit to end of row. (2 sts increased)
Increase rows (WS): Sl1k, knit to the first marker, sm, k to the second marker, sm, knit to end of row.

THUMB

After finishing Chart 1, work the sts of the thumb only. Place all sts on the outsides of the markers on a stitch holder. Don't cut the yarns attached to the main body of the mitten, as you can continue knitting with them for the second part of the mitten.

Using a new ball of C3, work from the RS as follows:
Row 1 (RS): K1, kfb, k until the end of the row. (1 st increased)
Row 2 (WS): Sl1k, k until the end of the row.
You now have **14 (16) 16 sts** for the thumb.
Row 3 (RS): Sl1k, k until the end of the row.
Row 4 (WS): Sl1k, k until the end of the row.
Repeat Rows 3 + 4 a further 6 (6) 7 times.

THUMB DECREASES

Size 1 only:
Row 1 (RS): Sl1k, repeat *k2tog, k1* to the last st, k1.
Row 2 (WS): Sl1k, k until the end of the row. You now have 10 sts in total.
Row 3 (RS): Sl1k, repeat *k2 tog, k1* to the end of the row.
Row 4 (WS): Repeat Row 2. You now have **7 sts** in total.

Sizes 2 + 3 only:
Row 1 (RS): Sl1k, repeat *k2tog, k1* to the end of the row.
Row 2 (WS): Sl1k, k until the end of the row. You now have 11 sts in total.
Row 3 (RS): Sl1k, repeat *k2tog, k1* until the last st, k1.
Row 4 (WS): Repeat Row 2 one more time. You now have **8 sts** in total.

Cut the yarn, leaving a tail of approx. 30cm (12in) for sewing. Thread the yarn through a tapestry needle and pass the needle through the remaining sts twice, beginning with the stitch on the opposite side of the thumb to your yarn. Sew the seam down the thumb using a version of mattress stitch that is suitable for garter stitch.

MITTEN TOP

Transfer the sts on the stitch holder back onto your needle to continue knitting the second part of the mitten. You need to pick up and knit 3 sts where the base of the thumb will join section 2 to avoid having a hole at that part. To do this, work as follows:

Row 1 (RS): Sl1k, k14 (16) 18, pick up and knit 3 sts below the thumb, k to the end of the row, changing the colours as per the previous row.
Row 2 (WS): Sl1k, k until the end of the row, changing the colours as per the previous row.
Continuing in garter stitch, begin working **Chart 2** (see pages 127–129) in your chosen size to knit the top part of the mitten.
Note: See page 123 for notes on reading the charts before you begin following Chart 2.

TOP DECREASES

After finishing Chart 2, you continue in garter stitch using C5 only to work the decreases of your mitten.
Row 1 (RS): K33 (37) 41 sts.
Row 2 (WS): Sl1k, k to end of row.
Row 3 (RS): Sl1k, repeat *k2tog, k 6 (7) 8* to the end of the row.
Row 4 (WS): Repeat Row 2. You now have **29 (33) 37 sts** in total.
Row 5 (RS): Sl1k, repeat *k3, k2tog, k 2 (3) 4* to the end of the row.
Row 6 (WS): Repeat Row 2. You now have **25 (29) 33 sts** in total.
Row 7 (RS): Sl1k, repeat *k2tog, k 4 (5) 6* to the end of the row.
Row 8 (WS): Repeat Row 2. You now have **21 (25) 29 sts** in total.
Row 9 (RS): Sl1k, repeat *k2, k2tog, k 1 (2) 3* to the end of the row.
Row 10 (WS): Repeat Row 2. You now have **17 (21) 25 sts** in total.
Row 11 (RS): Sl1k, repeat *k2tog, k 2 (3) 4* to the end of the row.
Row 12 (WS): Repeat Row 2. You now have **13 (17) 21 sts** in total.
Sizes 2 + 3 only:
Row 13 (RS): Sl1k, repeat *k1, k2tog, k - (1) 2* to the end of the row.
Row 14 (WS): Sl1k, k to end of row. You now have **- (13) 17 sts** in total.
Size 3 only:
Row 15 (RS): sl1k, repeat *k2tog, k - (-) 2* to the end of the row.
Row 16 (WS): Sl1k, k to end of row. You now have **- (-) 13 sts** in total.

SIDE SEAM
Cut C5, leaving a tail of approx. 30cm (12in) for sewing. Thread the yarn through a tapestry needle and pass the needle through the remaining sts twice, beginning with the stitch on the opposite side of the mitten to your yarn.

Sew the seam down the mitten, working from the RS and using the version of mattress stitch that is suitable for garter stitch. For an invisible seam, change colour while sewing to match the colour of the intarsia pattern.

SECOND MITTEN
The second mitten is created the same way as the first one, therefore repeat the instructions of the first mitten. To create a colourful contrast, substitute C3 for C4 and vice versa this time.

FINISHING
Weave in all ends, for example by using the duplicate stitch method on the WS of your work. Gently wash your Below The Horizon Mittens and block them according to the given measurements.

SIZE 1

- ☐ C1
- ☐ C2
- ☐ C3
- ☐ C4
- ☐ C5
- ☐ **ON RS AND WS ROW:** Knit st, instead of slip
- Ⅴ **KFB:** RS increase
- ☐ **GARTER EDGE STITCH**
- ← **CARRY YARN LEFT** See special techniques
- → **CARRY YARN RIGHT** See special techniques
- ✳ When cutting the working yarn, leave a tail of approx. 30cm (12in) for sewing

Note: See page 123 for notes on reading these charts before you begin following them.

CHART 2 MITTEN TOP

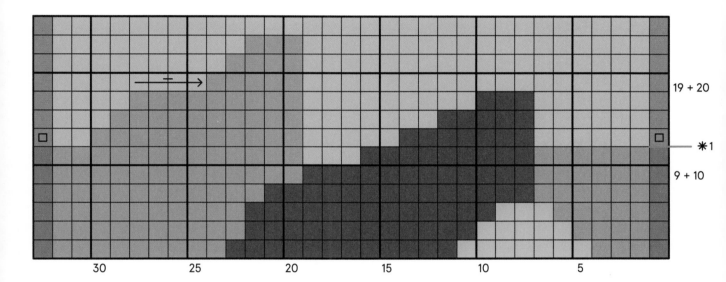

CHART 1 MITTEN BASE

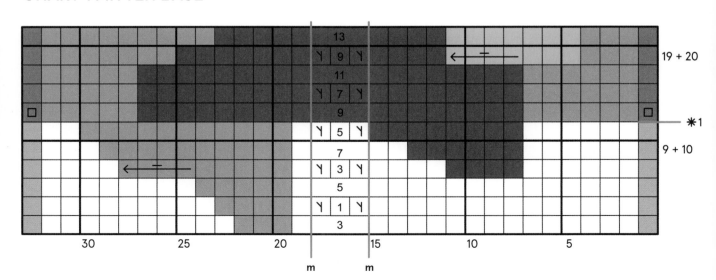

SIZE 2

See page 127 for key.

CHART 2 MITTEN TOP

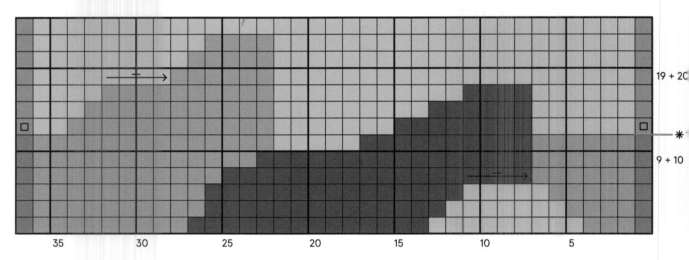

CHART 1 MITTEN BASE

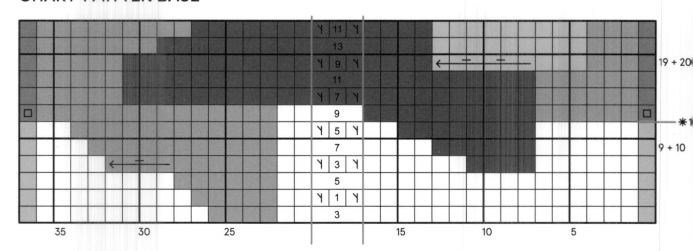

CHART 2 MITTEN TOP

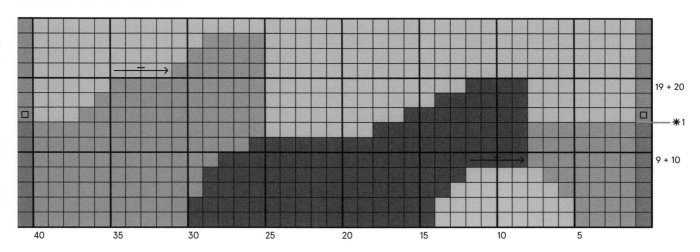

CHART 1 MITTEN BASE

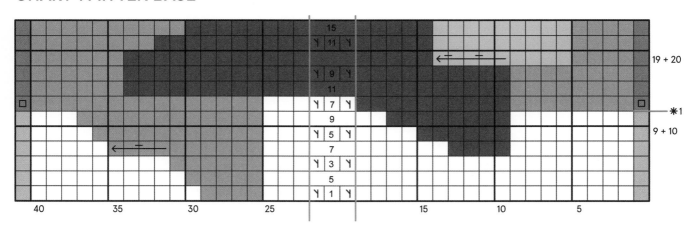

Dancing Sunbeams Sweater

The Dancing Sunbeams Sweater is inspired by my walks along a tiny path that makes the forest it winds through seem almost like a labyrinth. The place is most special during summer, when the ground is covered in fresh ferns and the canopy towers high above you. It feels like you are walking through a green tunnel. Then the sun suddenly appears, bathing the forest in a magical dappled light. Sunbeams sparkle through the branches, casting long shadows across the ground. As I walk along the path I cut through the rays of light, causing a fascinating dance of light and shade. It is this light-and-shadow play that I've captured in the intarsia motif for this sweater.

#dancingsunbeamssweater

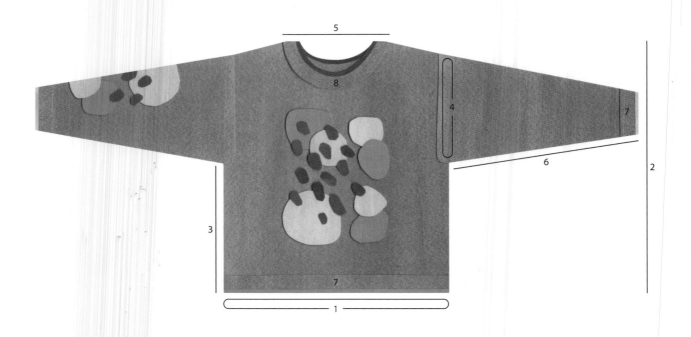

CONSTRUCTION

This sweater has a slightly retro shape and is knitted in garter stitch, using the intarsia technique to create an organic motif at the front and on the right sleeve.

The sweater is knitted from the top down. First, knit the back from the neckline to the point at the base where the ribbing will begin. Next, you pick up the stitches for the front and knit this side from the top down as well. The shoulder seam sits slightly towards the back, and both the front and the back shoulders are shaped with short rows. After finishing the front, work the bottom ribbing all the way around the garment in the round, then do the same for the neck ribbing. After this, you pick up and knit stitches for the sleeves, which are worked flat in garter stitch, with the ribs worked in the round. To finish the sweater, close the side seams and sleeve seams.

SKILL LEVEL
●●●●○

SIZES
Sizes 1 (2) 3 (4) 5 (6) 7 (8) 9 are designed to fit a bust circumference of: 76 (86) 96 (106) 116 (126) 136 (146) 156cm
/ 30 (34) 38 (42) 46 (50) 54 (57) 61in

The Dancing Sunbeams Sweater is designed to be worn with approx. 17–27cm (6¾–10½in) positive ease. Measure your bust circumference to choose a suitable size.

FINISHED MEASUREMENTS
1. **Bust circumference:** 98 (108) 118 (128) 138 (148) 158 (168) 178cm
   / 38½ (42½) 46½ (50½) 54¼ (58¼) 62¼ (66¼) 70in
2. **Total length:** 58 (59) 60 (60.5) 61.5 (62.5) 63 (64) 65cm
   / 22¾ (23¼) 23½ (23¾) 24¼ (24½) 24¾ (25¼) 25½in
3. **Length, bottom hem to armhole:** 31.5cm / 12½in
4. **Sleeve circumference, at widest point:** 45 (46) 48 (50) 52 (54) 56 (57) 58cm
   / 17¾ (18) 19 (19¾) 20½ (21¼) 22 (22½) 22¾in
5. **Neck width:** 20 (20) 21 (21) 22 (22) 23 (23) 24cm
   / 8 (8) 8¼ (8¼) 8¾ (8¾) 9 (9) 9½in
6. **Inside sleeve length:** 43.5 (42.5) 41.5 (40) 39 (38) 36 (35) 34.5cm
   / 13½ (16¾) 16¼ (15¾) 15¼ (15) 14¼ (13¾) 13½in
7. **Bottom and sleeve ribs:** Approx. 4.5cm / 1¾in
8. **Neck rib:** Approx. 3cm / 1¼in

Tip: If you wish to lengthen or shorten your sweater, see the advice on page 12.

YARN

Two strands of lace weight yarn held double or, alternatively, use one strand of a thicker 4-ply (fingering weight) or a 5-ply (sport weight) yarn. You will also need waste yarn for casting on.

Please note that these quantities are only estimates, and are for when using yarn held double. If using 1 strand, halve these quantities:

MC: 2834 (3075) 3315 (3510) 3816 (4082) 4323 (4563) 4823m
/ 3100 (3364) 3627 (3840) 4174 (4466) 4729 (4992) 5276yds
CC1: 124 (130) 137 (156) 163 (163) 183 (189) 196m
/ 136 (143) 150 (171) 178 (178) 200 (207) 214yds
CC2: 176 (176) 176 (196) 196 (196) 209 (215) 215m
/ (193) (193) 193 (214) 214 (214) 228 (235) 235yds
CC3: 130 (130) 137 (137) 137 (137) 143 (150) 150m
/ 143 (143) 150 (150) 150 (150) 157 (164) 164yds

Yarn used in the sample: La Bien Aimée Helix
(75 per cent Falkland Merino, 25 per cent Gotland Wool, 650m / 710yds – 100g / 3½oz), held double.
MC: Goldenrod, 5 (5) 6 (6) 6 (7) 7 (8) 8 skeins

La Bien Aimée Helix Mini Skein (75 per cent Falkland Merino, 25 per cent Gotland Wool, 163m / 178yds) – 25g / ⅞oz), held double.
CC1: Dawn, 1 (1) 1 (1) 1 (1) 2 (2) 2 skein(s)
CC3: Rust, 1 (1) 1 (1) 1 (1) 1 (1) 1 skein

La Bien Aimée Felix Mini Skein (75 per cent Falkland Merino, 25 per cent Corriedale, 163m / 178yds – 25g / ⅞oz), held double.
CC2: Peach Sweater, 2 (2) 2 (2) 2 (2) 2 (2) 2 skeins

NEEDLES

3mm (US 2.5) circular needles, or size needed to obtain the correct tension (gauge), for the body and 2.5mm (US 1.5) circular needles for the ribs.

TENSION (GAUGE)

25 sts x 45 rows to 10 x 10cm 4 x 4in) in garter stitch using MC held double, measured after washing and blocking.

READING THE CHARTS

The charts show only RS rows. The intarsia pattern for each odd-numbered row is exactly the same for the

following even-numbered row. So, for rows 1 and 2, read the chart row labelled 1 + 2 from right to left for row 1 (RS), then from left to right for row 2 (WS), and so on.

SPECIAL TECHNIQUES

INTARSIA JOIN
See pages 26–27.

PATTERN

BACK
First, knit the back of the sweater from the top down using a provisional cast on and shaping the shoulders by working German Short Rows.
Using 3mm (US 2.5) needles and waste yarn, cast on **120 (132) 145 (155) 168 (180) 193 (205) 218 sts** using a provisional cast-on method.

Row 1 (RS): Using MC, k to the end of the row.
Row 2 (WS): Sl1k, k to the end of the row.
Row 3 (RS): Sl1k, k 86 (92) 100 (106) 112 (119) 127 (133) 141 sts, turn.
Row 4 (WS): mDS, k 53 (53) 56 (58) 57 (59) 62 (62) 65 sts, turn.
Row 5 (RS): mDS, k to DS, kDS, k 3 (3) 3 (4) 4 (4) 4 (4) 4, turn.
Row 6 (WS): mDS, k to DS, kDS, k 3 (3) 3 (4) 4 (4) 4 (4) 4, turn.
Repeat Rows 5 + 6 a further 9 (11) 12 (10) 12 (13) 14 (16) 17 times, until there are 3 (3) 5 (4) 2 (4) 5 (3) 4 sts left until the end of the row.
Row 7 (RS): mDS, k to DS, kDS, k to the end of the row.
Row 8 (WS): Sl1k, k until DS, kDS, k to the end of the row.

ARMHOLES
Row 1 (RS): Sl1k, k to end of row.
Row 2 (WS): Repeat Row 1 one more time.
Repeat Rows 1 + 2 a further 35 (36) 36 (38) 38 (39) 39 (39) 40 times.
Armhole increases: Increase 1 st at the beginning and the end of each RS row as follows:
Row 1 (RS): Sl1k, k1, kfb, k until the last 3 sts, kfb, k2. (2 sts increased)
Row 2 (WS): Sl1k, k to end of row.

Repeat Rows 1 + 2 a further 1 (1) 1 (2) 2 (2) 2 (2) 2 time(s). You now have **124 (136) 149 (161) 174 (186) 199 (211) 224 sts** in total. Your work now measures approx. 22.2 (23.5) 24 (24.4) 25.3 (26.2) 26.7 (27.5) 28.5cm / 8¾ (9¼) 9½ (9½) 10 (10¼) 10½ (10¾) 11¼in from the cast-on edge, measured at the centre.

BODY
Row 1 (RS): Sl1k, k to end of row.
Row 2 (WS): Repeat Row 1.
Repeat Rows 1 + 2 a further 61 times until your work measures approx. 27.5cm (10¾in) from the armhole.

Cut the MC yarn, leaving a tail of approx. 1m (39½in) for sewing the side seams later.

Place all the stitches on a stitch holder. The bottom rib will be finished in the round when both the back and the front are finished.

FRONT
First, each shoulder is worked separately. The German Short Rows technique is used to shape the shoulders, beginning from the neckline edge. Next, stitches are increased at the neckline to shape the front neckline, then the stitches for the shoulders are joined together in the centre to knit the front with the intarsia motif.

LEFT SHOULDER
Begin by unravelling the provisional cast on. Transfer the first **36 (42) 47 (52) 58 (64) 69 (75) 80 sts** from the provisional cast on onto your working needle to knit the left shoulder, leaving **84 (90) 98 (103) 110 (116) 124 (130) 138 sts** on a stitch holder for the neck and the right shoulder.

Start working a RS row at the neckline, using 3mm (US 2.5) needles and MC.
Row 1 (RS): Using MC, k to the end of the row.
Row 2 (WS): Sl1k, k to the end of the row.
Row 3 (RS): Sl1k, k 2 (2) 2 (3) 3 (3) 3 (3) 3, turn.
Row 4 (WS): mDS, k to the end of the row.
Row 5 (RS): Sl1k, k to DS, kDS, k 3 (3) 3 (4) 4 (4) 4 (4) 4, turn.
Row 6 (WS): mDS, k to the end of the row.
Repeat Rows 5 + 6 a further 9 (11) 12 (10) 12 (13) 14 (16) 17 times, until there are 3 (3) 5 (4) 2 (4) 5 (3) 4 sts left until the end of the row.

Row 7 (RS): Sl1k, k to DS, kDS, k to the end of the row.

Row 8 (WS): Sl1k, k to the end of the row.

Row 9 (RS): Sl1k, k to the end of the row.

Row 10 (WS): Repeat Row 9.

Repeat Rows 9 + 10 a further 1 (1) 1 (1) 0 (0) 0 (0) 0 time(s).

LEFT NECK INCREASES

Stitches are now increased for the neckline at the beginning of every RS row after the first 2 stitches.

Row 1 (RS): Sl1k, k1, kfb, k to the end of the row. (1 st increased)

Row 2 (WS): Sl1k, k to the end of the row.

Repeat Rows 1 + 2 a further 11 (11) 12 (12) 12 (12) 13 (13) 14 times until you have **48 (54) 60 (65) 71 (77) 83 (89) 95 sts** in total. Cut MC and transfer all sts for the left shoulder to a stitch holder.

RIGHT SHOULDER

Transfer the first **36 (42) 47 (52) 58 (64) 69 (75) 80 sts** of the provisionally cast-on sts from the stitch holder to your needle. Leave the remaining **48 (48) 51 (51) 52 (52) 55 (55) 58 sts** on the stitch holder to work the back neck, for the neck rib.

Start working a RS row, using 3mm (US 2.5) needles and MC.

Row 1 (RS): Using MC, k to the end of the row.

Row 2 (WS): Sl1k, k to the end of the row.

Row 3 (RS): Sl1k, k to the end of the row.

Row 4 (WS): Sl1k, k 2 (2) 2 (3) 3 (3) 3 (3) 3, turn.

Row 5 (RS): mDS, k to the end of the row.

Row 6 (WS): Sl1k, k to DS, kDS, k 3 (3) 3 (4) 4 (4) 4 (4) 4, turn.

Repeat Rows 5 + 6 a further 9 (11) 12 (10) 12 (13) 14 (16) 17 times until there are 3 (3) 5 (4) 2 (4) 5 (3) 4 sts left until the end of the row.

Row 7 (RS): mDS, k to the end of the row.

Row 8 (WS): Sl1k, k to DS, kDS, k to the end of the row.

Row 9 (RS): Sl1k, k to the end of the row.

Row 10 (WS): Repeat Row 9.

Repeat Rows 9 + 10 a further 1 (1) 1 (1) 0 (0) 0 (0) 0 time(s).

RIGHT NECK INCREASES

Stitches are now increased for the neckline at the end of every RS row before the last 2 stitches.

Row 1 (RS): Sl1k, k to the last 4 sts, kfb, k3. (1 st increased)

Row 2 (WS): Sl1k, k to the end of the row.

Repeat Rows 1 + 2 a further 11 (11) 12 (12) 12 (12) 13 (13) 14 times until you have **48 (54) 60 (65) 71 (77) 83 (89) 95 sts** in total.

FRONT SECTION

Join both sets of shoulder stitches as follows:

Row 1 (RS): Sl1k, k to the end of the row, turn. Cast on **24 (24) 25 (25) 26 (26) 27 (27) 28 sts** from the wrong side using the knitted cast-on method. Turn back to the right side and continue working the left shoulder stitches from the stitch holder, knitting to the end of the row. You now have **120 (132) 145 (155) 168 (180) 193 (205) 218 sts** in total.

Row 2 (WS): Sl1k, k to the end of the row.

Row 3 (RS): Sl1k, k to the end of the row.

Row 4 (WS): Repeat Row 2 one more time.

Repeat Rows 3 + 4 a further 8 (9) 8 (8) 9 (9) 8 (8) 8 times, ensuring that, on the last repeat of Row 4, you place two markers within the row to indicate the beginning and the end of the stitches on which you will work the chart. Do this as follows: Sl1k, k 27 (33) 40 (42) 48 (54) 58 (64) 70, pm, k 64 (64) 64 (70) 70 (70) 76 (76) 76, pm, k 28 (34) 40 (42) 49 (55) 58 (64) 71.

At this point, begin working **Chart 1** (see pages 140–142) in your chosen size to create the intarsia pattern, *ensuring you work the armhole increases on the correct chart rows, as described below.*

Note: See page 133 for notes on reading the charts before you begin following Chart 1.

To keep the yarns from tangling, cut CC3 in short tails for each shape instead of knitting from multiple skeins at the same time. For the small shapes, you will need a CC3 tail measuring about 2m (2¼yds) and, for the larger shapes, you will need a CC3 tail measuring about 2.5m (2¾yds).

ARMHOLE INCREASES

On **Row 55 (55) 55 (63) 63 (65) 69 (69) 69** of **Chart 1** (depending on your chosen size), begin working armhole increases by increasing 1 stitch at the beginning and the end of each RS row as follows:

Row 1 (RS): Sl1k, k1, kfb, k to m, sm, k according to Chart 1 to m, sm, k to the last 3 sts, kfb, k2. (2 sts increased)

Row 2 (WS): Sl1k, k to m, sm, k according to Chart 1 to m, sm, k to end of row.

Repeat Rows 1 + 2 a further 1 (1) 1 (2) 2 (2) 2 (2) 2 time(s) while following the chart.

You now have **124 (136) 149 (161) 174 (186) 199 (211) 224 sts** in total.

Continue knitting in garter stitch with the edge stitch and follow Chart 1 in between your markers in your chosen size.

After finishing Chart 1, continue knitting in MC in plain garter stitch as follows:
Row 1 (RS): Sl1k, k to the end of the row.
Row 2 (WS): Repeat Row 1.
Repeat Rows 1 + 2 a further 18 (18) 18 (19) 19 (20) 18 (18) 18 times until the work measures approx. 27.5cm (10¾in) from the armhole.

BOTTOM RIBBING

Transfer all the back stitches from the stitch holder onto your needles so you can knit the bottom rib in the round. You will work a 1x1 rib. Using MC and 2.5mm (US 1.5) circular needles, work as follows:
Round 1: Knit all front sts and all back sts. Then, place a marker and join to work in the round. You now have **248 (272) 298 (322) 348 (372) 398 (422) 448 sts** in total.
Round 2: Repeat *k1, p1* across all sts.
Rounds 3–19: Repeat Round 2.
Round 20: Change to CC1 and repeat Round 2.
Round 21: Repeat *k1, sl1p wyif* across all sts.
Round 22: Repeat *sl1p wyib, p1* across all sts.

Cast (bind) off using your preferred method. This could, for example, be the Italian cast off or a stretchy sewn cast off variation worked as follows:
Cut off CC1, leaving a tail approx. 1.5 times longer than your circumference for binding off. Thread your yarn onto a tapestry needle.
Working from WS: Repeat *insert your tapestry needle purlwise into the first 3 sts on your left needle, coming out at the front. Drop the first st off the needle*, until the end of the round.

NECK RIBBING

Work a folded rib at the neckline using MC yarn. Begin by transferring the remaining stitches from the provisional cast on that are on the stitch holder back onto your needles.
Using 2.5mm (US 1.5) needles and MC, pick up and knit stitches as follows: beginning at the left side on the back,

after the held stitches from the cast on, repeat *(pick up and knit 1 st out of the garter edge stitch) 5 times, pick up and knit 1 st from between the garter edge stitches* for all the stitches up the side of the neckline. Then pick up and knit 1 st from every cast-on stitch at the front. Repeat the instructions for the neckline side stitches on the right and knit all the back neck stitches from the stitch holder. You now have **136 (142) 146 (148) 150 (152) 162 (166) 174 sts** in total.
Place a marker, join to work in the round and work the rib as follows:
Round 1: Repeat *k1, p1* to the end of round.
Rounds 2–12: Repeat Round 1.
Rounds 13 + 14: Change to CC3 and repeat Round 1.
Round 15: Repeat *k1, sl1p wyif* to the end of round.
Rounds 16 + 17: Repeat Round 15.
Rounds 18–21: Repeat Round 1.
Rounds 22–27: Change back to MC and repeat Round 1.
Before folding the rib and binding off, sew in the ends from the colour changes.

CAST (BIND) OFF

On the following round, fold the rib inwards, then secure the rib to the inside of the neckline by knitting every other stitch together with a stitch picked up from the beginning of the neck rib and binding off.
Tip: Turn the sweater inside out and work from the WS to make this process easier.
Work this round as follows:
K1, p1 and bind off 1 st. Repeat *pick up 1 st from the first row of the neck rib and place it onto your left needle, knit the st together with the next st on your left needle and bind off 1 st, p1 and bind off another st* to the end of the round.

LEFT SLEEVE

Working from the RS, begin at the armhole edge on the front of your sweater and work up along the front and then over the shoulder, then down along the back to the other armhole edge using MC and 3mm (US 2.5) needles. Work as follows: repeat *(pick up and knit 1 st out of the garter stitch edge stitch) 6 (5) 5 (5) 4 (4) 4 (3) 4 times, pick up and knit 1 st from between the garter edge stitches* until you have reached the end of the armhole and, at the end, pick up and knit a few extra stitches at the bottom of the armhole. You now have **114 (118) 122 (126) 130 (134) 140 (144) 146 sts.**

Set-up Row (WS): K to the end of the row.

Work in garter stitch as follows:

Row 1 (RS): Sl1k, k to the end of the row.

Row 2 (WS): Repeat Row 1.

Repeat Rows 1 + 2 a further 8 (3) 1 (0) 0 (1) 2 (0) 0 time(s).

SLEEVE DECREASES

Sizes 1–6 only: Decrease every 6th row as follows:

Row 1 (RS): Sl1k, k to the end of the row.

Rows 2–4: Repeat Row 1.

Row 5 (RS): Sl1k, k1, k2tog, knit to the last 4 sts, ssk, k2. (2 sts decreased)

Row 6 (WS): Repeat Row 1.

Repeat Rows 1–6 a further 25 (26) 26 (20) 16 (8) – (–) – times.

You now have **62 (64) 68 (84) 96 (116) – (–) – sts** remaining.

Sizes 4–6: Continue decreasing as described below.

Sizes 4–9 only: Decrease every 4th row as follows:

Row 1 (RS): Sl1k, k to the end of the row.

Row 2 (WS): Repeat Row 1.

Row 3 (RS): Sl1k, k1, k2tog, knit to the last 4 sts, ssk, k2. (2 sts decreased)

Row 4 (WS): Repeat Row 1.

Repeat Rows 1–4 a further – (–) – (7) 12 (22) 33 (33) 32 time(s).

You now have **– (–) – (68) 70 (70) 72 (76) 80 sts** remaining.

SLEEVE RIBBING

Work the rib in the round to match the bottom rib. Using 2.5mm (US 1.5) circular needles, work as follows:

Round 1: Knit all sts. Place a marker and join to work in the round.

Round 2: Repeat *k1, p1* to the end of round.

Rounds 3–17: Repeat Round 2.

Round 18: Change to CC2 and repeat Round 2.

Round 19: Repeat *k1, sl1p wyif* to the end of round.

Round 20: Repeat *sl1p wyib, p1* to the end of round.

Cast (bind) off using your preferred method, ie. the same as for the bottom rib. Remember to work the variation from the WS.

RIGHT SLEEVE

The right sleeve is worked as for the left sleeve, but is decorated with an intarsia motif. Working from the RS, begin at the armhole edge on the back of your sweater and work up along the back and then over the shoulder, then down along the front to the other armhole edge to pick up and knit the same number of stitches as for the left sleeve.

Follow the instructions for the decreases until you have worked 48 (44) 42 (38) 36 (40) 34 (32) 30 rows, counted from the picked up stitches.

CHART 2

At this point, begin working **Chart 2** (see page 143) in your chosen size, as outlined below and, *at the same time*, continue working the sleeve decreases as for the left sleeve. Ensure that, on the first row of **Chart 2**, you place two markers to indicate the beginning and the end of the chart as follows: mark out the centre of your sleeve and ensure that you have the same number of sts on the right side and left side of the centre, then count 14 (14) 14 (14) 14 (13) 13 (13) 13 sts to the left and place a marker, and then count 14 (14) 14 (14) 14 (13) 13 (13) 13 sts to the right of the centre and place a marker. Work Chart 2 in between the two markers.

As you did when working the motif at the front, cut CC3 in short tails for each shape for ease of knitting. You will need a CC3 tail measuring about 2m (2¼yds) for each of the shapes.

Note: See page 133 for notes on reading the charts before you begin following Chart 2.

After finishing Chart 2, continue working plain garter stitch, working the decreases as described for the left sleeve, for a further 32 (32) 30 (28) 26 (28) 26 (24) 22 rows.

SLEEVE RIBBING

Repeat the instructions as for the left sleeve to complete the right sleeve.

CLOSING THE SIDE AND SLEEVE SEAMS

Close both side seams by stitching together the front and back edges using the a version of mattress stitch that is suitable for garter stitch. Close the sleeve seams in the same way.

FINISHING

Sew in all remaining ends using the duplicate stitch method on the WS. Gently wash your Dancing Sunbeams Sweater and block it according to the measurements of your chosen size.

CHART 1 FRONT

SIZE 1–3

□ MC

■ CC1

■ CC2

■ CC3

— Beginning of armhole increases, see written instructions

Note: See page 133 for notes on reading the charts before you begin following them.

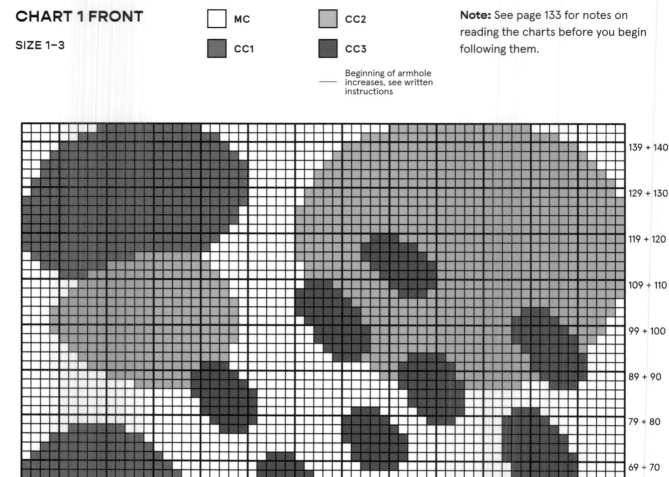
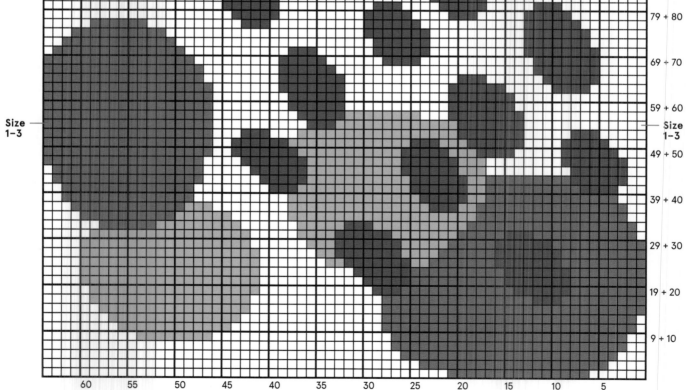

CHART 1 FRONT

SIZE 4-6

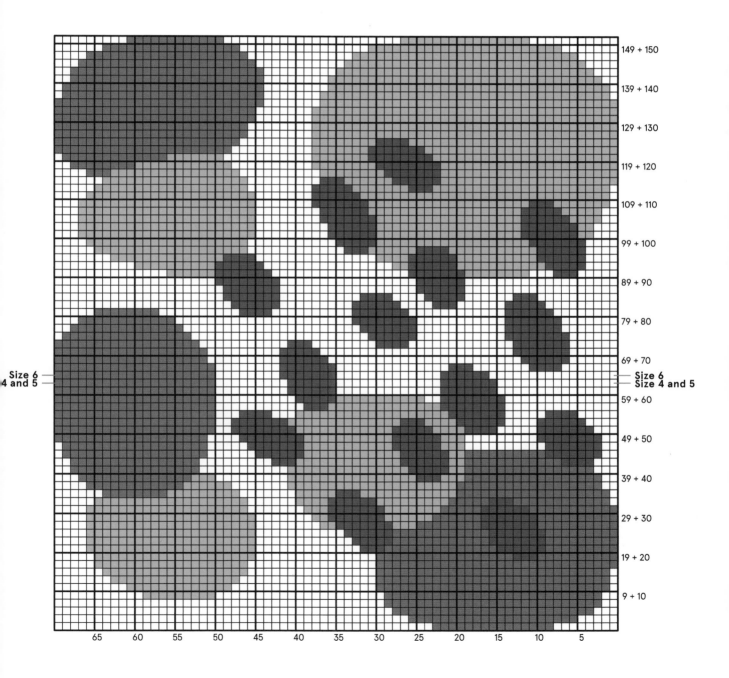

CHART 1 FRONT

SIZE 7–9   See page 140 for key.

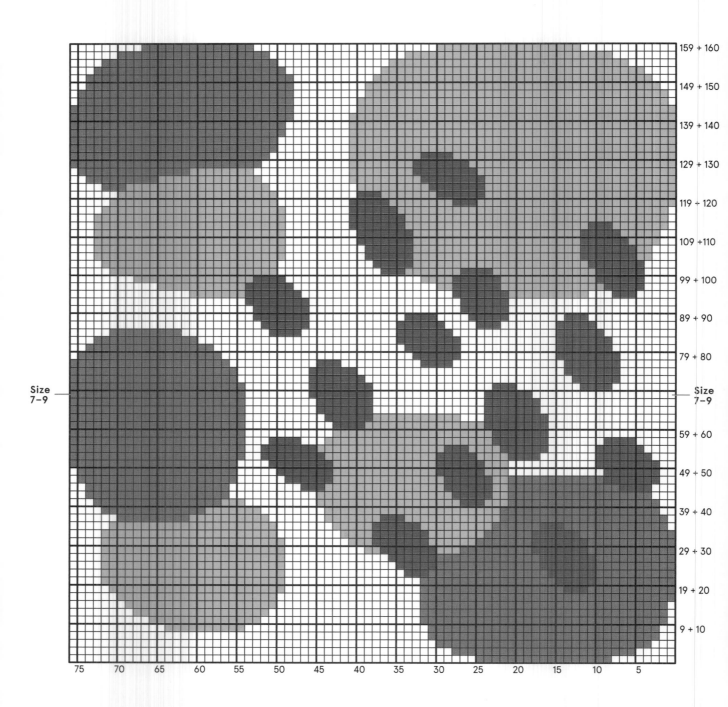

Dancing Sunbeams Sweater

CHART 2 RIGHT SLEEVE

SIZE 1–5

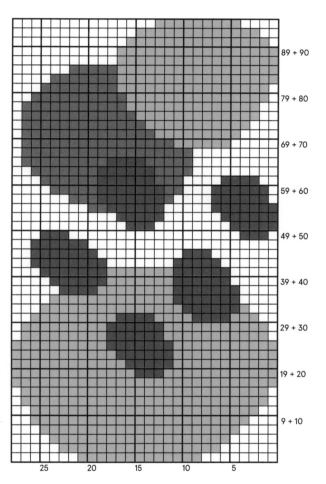

89 + 90
79 + 80
69 + 70
59 + 60
49 + 50
39 + 40
29 + 30
19 + 20
9 + 10

25 20 15 10 5

SIZE 6–9

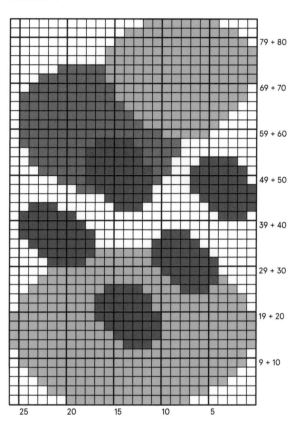

79 + 80
69 + 70
59 + 60
49 + 50
39 + 40
29 + 30
19 + 20
9 + 10

25 20 15 10 5

Floating on Water Scarf

The Floating On Water Scarf is inspired by a ferry ride you can take in the harbor of my hometown. I like the feeling of travelling on the water with the wind sweeping across my face while the landscape passes by. On one side of the river, you see the vibrant city and, on the opposite side, the cranes, the cruise ships in their shipyards, and many shipping containers that, together, form checkerboard patterns in countless colour combinations. My design for this scarf captures both the cheerful vibe of this ferry ride as well as the striking maritime scenery, which is reproduced abstractly in the motifs.

#floatingonwaterscarf

1

2

CONSTRUCTION

The Floating On Water Scarf is a skinny scarf knitted flat in garter stitch in combination with the intarsia technique. It is divided into three sections. Two are worked using pattern charts, creating graphic motifs at the beginning and the end of the scarf. Between the intarsia sections is a length of colour-block stripes. A small I-cord edge is worked along both sides throughout as you knit for neat edges. This edging follows the colour patterning of the motifs and stripes.

SKILL LEVEL
●○○○○

FINISHED MEASUREMENTS
1. **Length:** 174cm (68½in)
2. **Width:** 9cm (3½in)

The Floating On Water Scarf can easily be lengthened or shortened in the stripe section, just keep in mind that you will need to adjust your metreage/yardage (see below) according to your change.

YARN
One strand of bulky weight yarn in five shades.

C1: 87m (95yds)
C2: 27m (30yds)
C3: 24m (26yds)
C4: 65m (71yds)
C5: 47m (51yds)

Yarn used in the sample: Biches & Bûches, Le Coton & Alpaca (66 per cent GOTS Cotton and 34 per cent Super Fine Alpaca, 90m / 98yds – 50g / 1¾oz).
C1: Rose Grey, (1 skein)
C2: Light Grey Blue, (1 skein)
C3: Soft Dark Grey, (1 skein)
C4: Soft Gold, (1 skein)
C5: Dark Green Grey, (1 skein)

NEEDLES
4.5mm (US 7) straight or circular needles, or size needed to obtain the correct tension (gauge), and 5.5mm (US 9) needles for casting on.

TENSION (GAUGE)

18 sts x 34 rows (17 garter ridges) to 10 x 10cm (4 x 4in) in garter stitch, measured after washing and blocking.

READING THE CHARTS

Charts show only RS rows. The intarsia pattern for each odd-numbered row is exactly the same for the following even-numbered row. So, for rows 1 and 2, read the chart row labelled 1 + 2 from right to left for row 1 (RS), then from left to right for row 2 (WS), and so on.

SPECIAL TECHNIQUES

INTARSIA JOIN
See pages 26–27.

CARRYING YARNS AND BINDING FLOATS
See page 28–29.

I-CORD EDGE STITCH
First 2 sts of every row: K1, sl1p wyif.
Last 2 sts of every row: K1, sl1p wyif.

PATTERN

SECTION 1

Knit this first section with graphic motifs using the intarsia technique. To avoid the cast-on edge becoming too tight, cast on using the larger needle size.
Using 5.5mm (US 9) needles and C1, cast on **17 sts** using the long-tail cast-on method.
Change to 4.5mm (US 7) needles.
Set-up Row (WS): K1, sl1p wyif, k until there are 2 sts remaining, k1, sl1p wyif.

Begin working **Chart 1** (see page 148) to create the intarsia pattern and, *at the same time*, repeat **Rows 1 + 2** as follows:
Row 1 (RS): K1, sl1p wyif, k to the last 2 sts, k1, sl1p wyif.
Row 2 (WS): K1, sl1p wyif, k to the last 2 sts, k1, sl1p wyif.
Note: See above for notes on reading the charts before you begin following Chart 1.

SECTION 2

After completing Chart 1, continue working a colour-block stripe section in plain garter stitch as follows. Using C4, work as follows:
Row 1 (RS): K1, sl1p wyif, k to the last 2 sts, k1, sl1p wyif.
Row 2 (WS): K1, sl1p wyif, k to the last 2 sts, k1, sl1p wyif.
Repeat Rows 1 + 2 a further 15 times, for 16 garter stitch ridges in total.
Using **C5**, **repeat Rows 1 + 2** as above a further 10 times.
Using **C1**, **repeat Rows 1 + 2** as above a further 32 times.
Using **C3**, **repeat Rows 1 + 2** as above a further 16 times.
Using **C2**, **repeat Rows 1 + 2** as above a further 10 times.
Using **C4**, **repeat Rows 1 + 2** as above a further 10 times.
Using **C5**, **repeat Rows 1 + 2** as above a further 16 times.
Using **C1**, **repeat Rows 1 + 2** as above a further 22 times.

SECTION 3

Knit this third section with graphic motifs using the intarsia technique.

Using C4, begin working **Chart 2** (see page 148) to create the intarsia pattern and, *at the same time*, repeat **Rows 1 + 2** as follows:
Row 1 (RS): K1, sl1p wyif, k to the last 2 sts, k1, sl1p wyif.
Row 2 (WS): K1, sl1p wyif, k to the last 2 sts, k1, sl1p wyif.
Note: See left for notes on reading the charts before you begin following Chart 2.

CAST (BIND) OFF

After completing Chart 2, cast off all stitches as follows:
K1, p1, cast off 1 st, repeat *k1, bind off 1 st* to the end of the row.

FINISHING

Weave in all ends, for example by using the duplicate stitch method on the WS of your work. Gently wash your Floating On Water Scarf and block it according to the measurements.

Note: See page 147 for notes on reading these charts before you begin following them.

CHART 1 SECTION 1

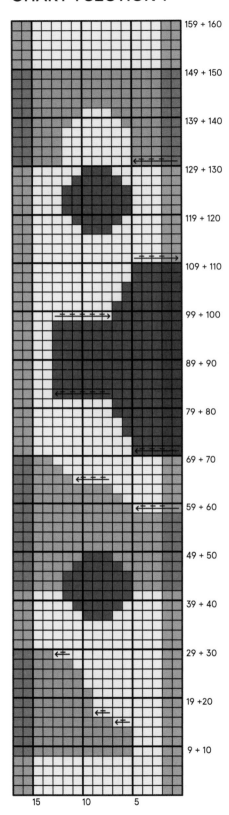

CHART 2 SECTION 3

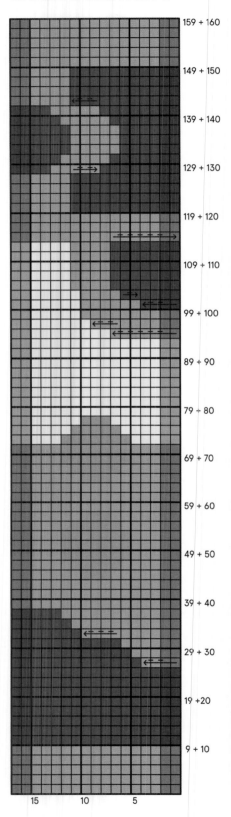

- ☐ C1
- ☐ C2
- ☐ C3
- ☐ C4
- ☐ C5
- ☐☐ I-CORD EDGE STITCH
- ← CARRY YARN LEFT
  See special techniques
- → CARRY YARN RIGHT
  See special techniques

Full of Flowers Bag

My hometown is a large, noisy, hectic city, but between the built-up areas you can find wildflower meadows, planted for the benefit of biodiversity and as sources of shelter and food for wildlife. I am fascinated by these little oases of natural life. If you look closely, they provide endless inspiration for shapes and colour combinations. The texture and motif of the Full of Flowers Bag are reminiscent of the small flower petals and leaves I find in these meadows, and also capture something of the essence of these beautiful habitats in an abstract way.

#fullofflowersbag

FLAT UNFINISHED

FINISHED FROM EITHER SIDE

CONSTRUCTION

The Full of Flowers Bag is worked flat in a slip stitch pattern that creates a firm, textured fabric that is suitable for bags. The intarsia technique is also used, creating four graphic shapes.

The Full of Flowers Bag is knitted from the top down, decreasing stitches at the bottom to create the half-moon shape. Knit both sides of the bag separately and join them with a 3-needle cast (bind) off at the bottom. Sew together the side seams and attach a zipper and cotton ribbon to hide the zipper seam.

An optional wrist strap is worked as a long, narrow rectangle in the same slip stitch pattern used for the bag, then joined at the long edges to form a tube. A caribiner is slipped onto the length before it is joined in a loop. The caribiner hooks onto the hole in the zipper's pull tab to attach the strap to the bag.

SKILL LEVEL
●●●○○

FINISHED MEASUREMENTS

This bag can be knitted in various weights of yarn, such as 4-ply (fingering weight), DK (light worsted) or aran (worsted), resulting in various sizes despite using the same pattern.

Measurements of the finished bag in the suggested yarns:
1. **Length:** 22cm (8½in)
2. **Width:** 14.5cm (5¾in)

YARN

Two strands of light 4-ply (fingering weight) yarn held double or, alternatively, use one strand of a heavier 5-ply (sport weight) yarn. For the motifs, use up some leftovers, for example 3 strands of lace weight yarn held together.

These quantities are for if you are using MC and CC1 held double, and CC2, CC3 and CC4 held triple. If using single strands, halve the quantities for MC and CC1, and use one-third of the quantities for CC2, CC3 and CC4.

MC: 156m (171yds)
CC1: 117m (128yds)
CC2: 30m (33yds)
CC3: 30m (33yds)
CC4: 30m (33yds)

Yarn required for the wrist strap:
MC: 32m (35yds)
CC1: 26m (29yds)

Yarn used in the sample: G-uld, No. 4 Mini (75 per cent wool - Falkland, 25 per cent wool - Gotland, 162m / 177yds – 25g / ⅞oz), held double.
MC: Walnut, G1 (1 skein)
CC1: Heather & Indigo, G2 (1 skein)

G-uld, Embroidery Wool (100 per cent wool, 40m / 44yds – 4g / ⅛oz), held triple.
CC2: Fern, B2 (1 skein)
CC3: Madder root B4 (1 skein)
CC4: Indigo, B4 (1 skein)

ZIPPER & CARABINER
Use a zipper suitable for the size of your finished purse. Zipper for the suggested yarn: 21cm (8¼in) long.
Small carabiner.

COTTON RIBBON
1.5cm (½in) wide, approx 50cm (19½in) long, or to suit the size of the finished bag.

NEEDLES
4mm (US 6) circular needles, or size needed to obtain correct tension (gauge), plus a separate needle in the same size for the 3-needle cast (bind) off.

TENSION (GAUGE)
30 sts x 31 rows to 10 x 10cm (4 x 4in) in the 2-coloured slip stitch pattern, measured after washing and blocking.

Knit a swatch in the slip stitch pattern (see right) to determine which needle size you need to achieve the correct tension. For the tension swatch, work the slip stitch pattern as follows:
Cast on an odd number of sts using the long-tail cast-on method and MC.
Set-up Row MC (WS): P2, repeat *sl1p wyif, p1* to the last 3 sts, sl1p wyif, p2.
Row 1 CC (RS): Sl2p wyib, repeat *k1, sl1p wyib* to the last 3 sts, k1, sl2p wyib.
Row 2 CC (WS): Sl2p wyif, repeat *k1, sl1p wyif* to the last 3 sts, k1, sl2p wyif.
Row 3 MC (RS): K2, repeat *sl1p wyib, k1* to the last 3 sts, sl1p wyib, k2.
Row 4 MC (WS): P2, repeat *sl1p wyif, p1* to the last 3 sts, sl1p wyif, p2.
Repeat Rows 1–4 until your swatch is large enough to check the tension.

READING THE CHARTS
One chart row represents 4 knitted rows – corresponding to one set (rows 1–4) of the repeated 4-row slip stitch pattern. Each chart row shows Row 1 (CC RS rows) of the slip stitch pattern. *This is the only row in each set of 4 rows in which the intarsia colour changes occur*. Read rows 1 and 3 of the slip stitch pattern from right to left, and rows 2 and 4 from left to right. Narrow boxes indicate sts worked in MC, while wider boxes represent sts worked in CC yarns. Diagonal lines at the chart edges indicate that decreases occur on the *third* row of the 4-row slip stitch pattern represented by that chart row.

ADDITIONAL ABBREVIATIONS
sssk: slip 1 st knitwise, slip the next two sts together knitwise, knit all 3 slipped sts together through the back loop. (2 sts decreased)

k3tog: work a ssk, slip this stitch back onto the left needle and pass the following st over. Slip the st back onto your right needle. (2 sts decreased)

sssk–k2tog: work a sssk, then k2tog and pass the sssk over this stitch. (4 sts decreased)

ssk–ssk: work a ssk twice and pass the second stitch over the first. Slip this stitch back onto the left needle and pass the following stitch over. Slip the stitch back onto your right needle. (4 sts decreased)

SPECIAL TECHNIQUES

INTARSIA JOIN
See pages 26–27.

SLIP STITCH PATTERN
The slip stitch pattern combines a garter stitch background with vertical lines in stocking (stockinette) stitch. The vertical lines are worked in MC only (and are represented by the narrow boxes in the charts), while the background is knitted with four different CC shades to create the intarsia motif. When slipping the stitches, hold the working yarn on the WS of the work.
This slip stitch pattern is worked over 4 rows. Remember that:
CC rows (Rows 1 + 2) are rows in which only CC yarns are knitted, and therefore your working yarn is always one of the CC yarns. All MC sts you come accross on CC rows will be slipped.
MC rows (Rows 3 + 4) are rows in which only MC sts are either knitted or purled, and therefore your working yarn is always MC. All CC sts you come accross in these rows will be slipped.

PATTERN

SECTION 1

First, knit one side of the bag working the slip stitch pattern throughout, and making decreases at the bottom to shape the bag.

Using MC, cast on **67 sts** using the long-tail cast-on method.

Set-up Row (WS): P2, repeat *sl1p wyif, p1* to the last 3 sts, sl1p wyif, p2.

Begin working **Chart 1** (see page 157) to create the intarsia colour pattern and, *at the same time*, **repeat Rows 1–4** as follows to work the slip stitch pattern:

Row 1 CC (RS): Sl2p wyib, repeat *k1, sl1p wyib* to the last 3 sts, k1, sl2p wyib.

Row 2 CC (WS): Sl2p wyif, repeat *k1, sl1p wyif* to the last 3 sts, k1, sl2p wyif.

Row 3 MC (RS): K2, repeat *sl1p wyib, k1* to the last 3 sts, sl1p wyib, k2.

Row 4 MC (WS): P2, repeat *sl1p wyif, p1* to the last 3 sts, sl1p wyif, p2.

Note: See page 153 for notes on reading the charts before you begin following Chart 1.

DECREASE ROWS

To create the half-moon shape, decrease 2 sts at the beginning and the end of **Rows 59, 67, 75, 79 and 83 of Chart 1** (which are all Row 3 of the slip stitch pattern established above, and MC RS rows). To do so, replace Row 3 of the slip stitch pattern with the decrease row below:

Decrease Row 3 MC (RS): K2, sl1p wyib, sssk, repeat *sl1p wyib, k1* to the last 7 sts, sl1p wyib, k3tog, sl1p wyib, k2. (4 stitches decreased)

To continue creating the half-moon shape, decrease 4 sts at the beginning and end of **Rows 87** and **91 of Chart 1** (which, again, are all Row 3 of the slip stitch pattern established above and MC RS rows). To do so, replace Row 3 of the slip stitch pattern with the decrease row below:

Decrease Row 3 MC (RS): K2, sl1p wyib, sssk–k2tog, repeat *sl1p wyib, k1* to the last 9 sts, sl1p wyib, ssk–ssk, sl1p wyib, k2. (8 stitches decreased)

Following the last CC rows of the chart and the MC RS row, work the last MC WS row as follows:

Row 92 MC (WS): P2tog, repeat *sl1p wyif, p1* to the last 3 sts, sl1p wyif, p2tog.

You now have **29 sts** in total. Break both yarns and place all stitches on a stitch holder.

SECTION 2

The second side of the bag is knitted the same way as the first. Repeat the instructions for Section 1, but instead of following Chart 1 as described, follow **Chart 2** (see page 157) instead.

CAST (BIND) OFF

You now have the sts for section 2 on your right needle. Transfer the stitches for Section 1 onto your left needle. Hold both needles together so that the RS of the bag sections are facing each other and the WS are facing outwards. Using MC and a separate needle, finish the bottom seam by working a 3-needle cast off as follows: knit 1 st from the front needle and 1 st from the back needle together. Now repeat: *knit 1 st from the front needle and 1 st from the back needle together and bind off 1 st* to the end of the row.

SIDE SEAMS

Using mattress stitch, sew together both side seams to join Sections 1 and 2.

FINISHING

Sew in all ends, for example by using the duplicate stitch method on the WS. Gently wash your Full of Flowers Bag and block it according to the measurements.

ZIPPER

Sew in the zipper by hand, using a sewing thread that matches MC. With the zipper closed, pin both ends of the zipper into the corners of the bag. Then, open the zipper and pin it in place along the sides of the bag with the cast-on edge aligned with the teeth of the zipper. To make sewing easier, you can secure the zipper by tacking (basting) stitches along the opening first, so that you can remove all the pins.

Next, sew the ribbon of the zipper onto your bag by backstitching right below your cast-on stitches.

To neaten the inside of your bag, you can choose to add a cotton ribbon to hide the zipper. Start at one corner by sewing the top edge of the ribbon onto your zipper ribbon, covering the seam. When you have sewn all around the top edge, cut the end of your ribbon, leaving an about 2.5cm (1in) piece. Fold it inwards and sew it on top of the beginning of the ribbon. Now, sew the bottom edge of the ribbon onto your bag as well.

WRIST STRAP (OPTIONAL)

You can add a wrist strap for wearing your Full Of Flowers Bag as a clutch. Work using MC and the CC of your choice as follows.

Using MC, cast on **11 sts** using the long-tail cast-on method.

Set-up Row MC (WS): P2, repeat *sl1p wyif, p1* to the last 3 sts, sl1p wyif, p2.

Row 1 CC (RS): Sl2p wyib, repeat *k1, sl1p wyib* to the last 3 sts, k1, sl2p wyib.

Row 2 CC (WS): Sl2p wyif, repeat *k1, sl1p wyif* to the last 3 sts, k1, sl2p wyif.

Row 3 MC (RS): K2, repeat *sl1p wyib, k1* to the last 3 sts, sl1p wyib, k2.

Row 4 MC (WS): P2, repeat *sl1p wyif, p1* to the last 3 sts, sl1p wyif, p2.

Repeat Rows 1–4 a further 40 times, or until the strap reaches your preferred length.

Cut CC and cast (bind) off all sts using MC. Cut MC leaving a tail of approx. 1m (39¼in) for sewing.

Weave in all ends not used for sewing on the WS. Sew the long edges together using mattress stitch to create a long tube.

Thread your carabiner hook onto the tube and sew together the cast-on and cast-off edge to create a loop. Be careful not to twist the tube when sewing it together.

With the side seam on the inside, slide the carabiner approx. 2.5cm (1in) away from your cast-on/cast-off seam. Wrap a length of MC around the two parts of your loop adjacent to the carabiner to secure it at one end of the loop and hide the cast-on/cast-off seam under the wrap at the same time. Secure MC and weave in the end.

■ MC	■ CC3
■ CC1	□ CC4
■ CC2	

Note: See page 153 for notes on reading these charts before you begin following them.

CHART 2 SECTION 2

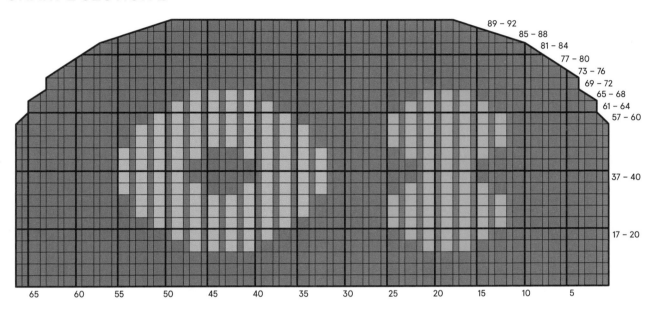

CHART 1 SECTION 1

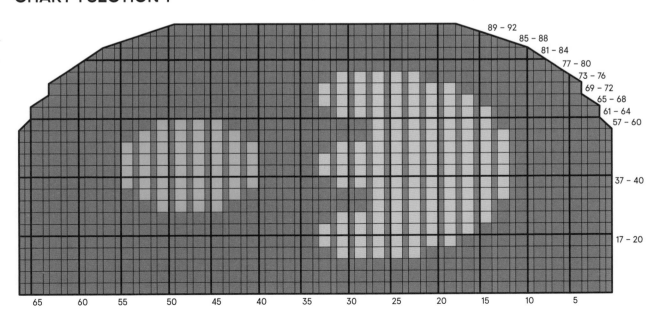

Resources

Many thanks to the following companies who kindly sponsored yarns to knit the designs in this book and who sponsored tools and garments for the photoshoot.

YARNS USED IN THE PROJECTS:

- Felix and Helix by La Bien Aimée (labienaimee.com)
- Svensk Ull 3 tr by Järbo (jarbo.se)
- Soft Silk Mohair and Pure Silk by Knitting for Olive (knittingforolive.com)
- Kinu by ITO (ito-yarn.com)
- Knit By Numbers 4ply by John Arbon Textiles (jarbon.com)
- Le Coton & Alpaca by Biches & Bûches (bichesetbuches.com)
- Robinson by De Rerum Natura (dererumnatura.fr)
- No. 4 and Embroidery Wool by G-uld (g-uld.dk)
- Snefnug by CaMaRose (camarose.dk)
- Undine by Ritual Dyes (ritualdyes.com)

TOOLS AND GARMENTS PROVIDED FOR THE SHOOT:

- Knitter's Block Kit, Maker's Board and Ruler & Gauge Set by Cocoknits (cocoknits.com)
- Wrap skirt, quilted jacket and pants by Linen-ID (linenid.com)
- Pants, sweatshirt and t-shirt by Colorful Standard (colorfulstandard.com)
- Blocking wire set by Lazadas Knit (lazadas.net)

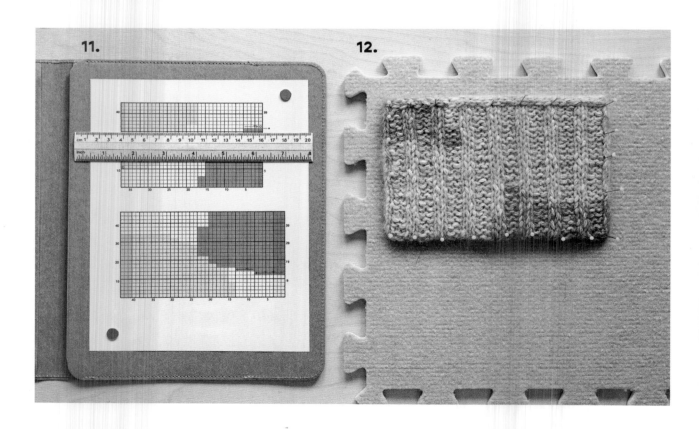

11.

12.

About the author

Anna Husemann is a textile and knitwear designer, who runs a small business selling colourful and eco-friendly knit accessories, knitwear designs and knitting patterns. She lives in Hamburg, Germany, together with her partner and their little cat Katzi, who is her diligent assistant – whatever Anna is working on she wants to be part of, sit on or play with.

You can follow Anna's work on Instagram via @anna_husemann

Acknowledgements

I would like to say thank you to everyone who has contributed to this book and has supported me creating it.

Many thanks to the lovely team at Quadrille for believing in my work and for giving me the opportunity to create a book about it: editors Ore and Harriet for your trust in me throughout the entire process, designers Alicia and Gemma for bringing all the ideas together in a layout and copyeditor Salima for your patience with polishing my text and the knitting patterns.

Thank you, Lena, for your patience during the shoot and for capturing my creations this atmospherically, and to Lotta for your colourful expertise.

Many thanks to Johanna and Anke, not only for agreeing to model my projects with me and to knit your own samples, but also for infecting me with your excitement. Thanks a lot, Emalie, for looking at the patterns in their first stage and for sorting my thoughts.

And many thanks to all my lovely test knitters for your enthusiasm about the intarsia technique and your helpful feedback on the patterns.

Thank you, Martina and Maren, for your thoughts and chats about the book and for your time knitting a sample. And thanks a lot, Catherine and Michael as well as Steffen and Sara, for your support and interest in the process.

Thanks a lot, my dear Max, for all your patience throughout: for listening to my ideas and thoughts, looking at all the colours and designs and for brainstorming with me. Thank you for having my back, for all your encouraging words when I was in doubt and for your ideas when I didn't know what to do. It means everything to me that you support me in any way!

And lastly, thank you my dear Gitti, for always supporting me and listening to my thoughts and concerns about my work. I wish I could show you this book and would love to know what you think about it.

Managing Director
Sarah Lavelle
Editorial Director
Harriet Butt
Assistant Editor
Oreolu Grillo
Art Director & Designer
Alicia House
Senior Designer
Gemma Hayden
Copyeditor
Salima Hirani
Photographer
Lena Scherer
Stylist
Lotta Meyer
Hair & Make-up
Bernadett Niedhardt
Models
Anna, Johanna and Anke
Head of Production
Stephen Lang
Production Controller
Martina Georgieva

Published in 2024 by
Quadrille Publishing Limited

Quadrille
52–54 Southwark Street
London SE1 1UN
quadrille.com

Text © Anna Husemann 2024
Photography © Lena Scherer 2024
except page 158 © Anna Husemann 2024
Illustrations © Anna Husemann 2024
Design © Quadrille 2024

ISBN 978 1 8378 3151 7

Printed in China